EDWARD KENNEDY

Books by Murray B. Levin

The Alienated Voter: Politics in Boston

The Compleat Politician: Political Strategy
in Massachusetts

Kennedy Campaigning: The System and the Style
as Practiced by Senator Edward Kennedy

Political Hysteria in America: The Democratic
Capacity for Repression

Edward Kennedy: The Myth of Leadership
(with T. A. Repak)

EDWARD KENNEDY

The Myth of Leadership

MURRAY B. LEVIN

AND

T. A. REPAK

BOSTON

HOUGHTON MIFFLIN COMPANY

1980

For Cope

MBL

For Damaris

TAR

Library of Congress Cataloging in Publication Data
Levin, Murray Burton.   Edward Kennedy.
1. Kennedy, Edward Moore, 1932–   2. Presidents —
United States — Election — 1980–   3. United States —
Politics and government — 1945–   I. Repak, T. A., joint author.
E840.8.K35L48   973.92'092'4   [B]   80-13277
ISBN 0-395-29249-2

Printed in the United States of America

V 10 9 8 7 6 5 4 3 2 1

Contents

Introduction

"HE TAUGHT ME to ride a bicycle, throw a forward pass, and sail against the wind." The *New York Times* reported that Edward Kennedy spoke "without self-pity and without tears." It was the opening of the John F. Kennedy Memorial Library. Many wept as he evoked the image of his brother. "It was all so brief, those thousand days are like an evening gone. But they are not forgotten . . . We can recall those years of grace, that time of hope, the spark still glows, the journey never ends, the dream shall never die."

Historians may designate this as the day Edward Kennedy symbolically announced his candidacy for the presidency of the United States, though he made the formal announcement in Faneuil Hall, that ancient and beautiful building so intimately associated with the American heritage.

The millions who loved John Kennedy harbor a hope that Edward Kennedy will resume the journey and fulfill the dream. If the polls before the events in Iran were reliable, there was substance to that dream.

This is, in part, a book about Edward Kennedy, his senatorial politics, his position on great issues, and the quality of his leadership. It is a book about the Kennedy campaign system, and the manner in which the Kennedy machine is deployed. It is also about Edward Kennedy's character, his morality, and his alleged charisma. These topics may be of critical interest to the American voter, whose involvement in the legend of Camelot or the events at Chappaquiddick may exceed his concern for issues. The outcome of this election may turn on America's assessment of Kennedy's character and the Kennedy mystique. In mid to late 1979, political writers thought that Kennedy had an important advantage because, as a candidate, he offered the promise of a symbolic resurrection, a resurrection that might expiate the guilt and sorrow felt at the death of John Kennedy. Kennedy's character and personal behavior, therefore, are central concerns, both in terms of how they may affect the preference of voters and of Kennedy's own behavior if elected.

But Kennedy has served in the Senate for seventeen years and he has a public record as well as a private life. We deal with that record in depth, particularly in the area of national health insurance, foreign policy, and judicial reform.

But our concern extends beyond Kennedy and the 1980 campaign. The campaign and the candidates can only be understood within the wider setting of American politics, and therefore we deal with the behavior of the American voter, the politics of national nominating conventions, problems of political strategy and fund raising, and the issue of whether a Kennedy presidency might make a difference.

To evaluate whether Edward Kennedy, as President, would seek qualitative social change, an elevation of communal rights coupled with limits on private action, we examine traditional American political values and Kennedy's willingness to break with the American past.

Few incumbent Presidents of the United States have been opposed for renomination. Kennedy challenged Carter because the Presidents' record on domestic affairs was so dismal and his standing in the polls so low. Kennedy challenged Carter, in other words, because the senator thought he could win. If the Kennedy mystique has ended, one must understand how Carter developed a campaign strategy that successfully masked his incompetence in domestic politics and contributed to the stigma of Chappaquiddick. Carter, as well as Kennedy, is our concern.

We began this book in August 1979, when the ayotallah was an obscure religious figure and the polls indicated that Kennedy was leading Carter by a margin of two to one. We completed our work shortly after the caucauses were held in Iowa in January 1980. The charisma of John Kennedy appears to be nontransferable. The power and prestige of an incumbent President appears formidable, particularly when the international situation is turbulent.

We could not have completed this volume without the help of Ellie Squire, Larry Goldbaum, Mary Perry, Joseph Kessler, and Marta Mestrovic, who were most willing to type while others slept.

T. A. Repak wrote chapters 3, 4, 5, and 6. Murray Levin wrote chapters 1, 2, 7, 8, and 9.

Murray B. Levin
T. A. Repak
February 1980

EDWARD KENNEDY

1

Edward Kennedy
and the American Dream

EDWARD KENNEDY is heir to a myth, yet he must deal with his personal and political reality. Sons of famous fathers and brothers of famous brothers do not stand by themselves, for they are filial and fraternal before they are themselves. Edward Kennedy is not only Edward Kennedy. He is the brother of a martyred president, and himself a candidate for that elusive office; he is the brother of a man who also sought that office and was murdered at gunpoint. Edward Kennedy is certainly a unique figure in American politics. He is the only man ever to become a senator while his brother was President. He is the son of one of the more shrewd entrepreneurs of this century and has inherited a great fortune. He is not only the youngest and most pampered son of a religious and formidable mother, but the youngest of nine siblings. It cannot be easy for *him*, let alone the public, to separate his mythic past from his present reality.

He says that he wants to be judged by his own work in the Senate, yet he invokes the Camelot legend and plays upon the Kennedy charisma. And his election to the Senate came about in large part because he was the President's brother. He says he is Edward Kennedy, and independent, but it is the Kennedy money that permits him to hire the largest staff in the Senate, and it is the clan's charisma that excites his audience. He cannot stand alone because, more than most men, he is perceived as a reflection of others. To understand who he is, or they are, one must analyze the myth.

For many, the Kennedy family is the American Dream come true, the triumph of Horatio Alger against unbelievable odds. But this image must be tempered by the facts. When Joseph Kennedy married Rose Fitzgerald, his father was neither poor nor unknown in the Boston community. And when Rose Fitzgerald married Joseph Kennedy, her father was the affable and affluent mayor of Boston. Unlike many other sons of the Boston Irish, Joseph Kennedy did not work as an unskilled laborer after high school; he attended Harvard. Rose Fitzgerald was neither a domestic servant nor a shopgirl. She was an Irish debutante.

The Kennedys and the Fitzgeralds were, however, Irish, and this meant that in Boston at the turn of the century they were members of a minority, albeit a minority on the verge of transcending half a decade of oppression. For Boston, the home of the bean and the cod, the city of the Lowells and Cabots, was governed by an entrenched Protestant elite that held a monopoly of economic and political power and systematically excluded the Irish from their society, their economy, and their political ranks. The symbol of the era was the infamous sign "Irish need not apply." Once the great Irish immigration of the mid-nineteenth century began, however, it was only a matter of time before the Irish immigrants were politically organized, the Irish machine established, and city hall fell to the Fitzgeralds and the Curleys.

The Irish arrived by thousands and tens of thousands, and true to legend, they came hungry, poor, and with little to lose. The unremitting struggle for subsistence in Ireland in the mid-nineteenth century condemned almost every Irish family to a bleak existence in which starvation was an immediate possibility. In Ireland in the eighteen forties, even a hearty potato crop barely nourished hardworking farmers. Thousands of children suffered from malnutrition while the majority of the population hovered on the verge of subsistence. In 1845 the potato crop was destroyed by blight, and famine and disease ravaged the nation. The only escape seemed to be America, an Irish dream. The trickle of immigration soon turned into a flood, and Boston became Celtic as well as Brahmin.

Like most of his countrymen, Patrick Kennedy, Sr., found conditions in Ireland unpromising. He was not a poor and inelegant peasant like most of his neighbors, and he had the energy and the resources to consider a move to America. The Kennedy biographer, James MacGregor Burns, wrote of Patrick Kennedy's origins: "Patrick Joseph Kennedy, of county Wexford, lived in a region of Ireland that had escaped the worst of the terrible potato famine. Less out of desperation than ambition, he decided to strike out for the new world of opportunities . . . Because of skills learned in the old country, he soon found employment as a cooper and a home in a somewhat better part of Boston than the squalid sections where most of the Irish lived."

Life in Boston at the time was little better than in Ireland. Thousands of immigrants lived in basements and tiny garrets in South Boston, barely surviving in filth and squalor, freezing in the bitter winter cold and constantly at war with vermin and fetid air. Extended families of ten and twelve lived like caged animals in rooms designed for three or four. Cholera and smallpox were common, and working conditions were harsh. It was not unusual for immigrants to work fifteen hours a day and seven days a week. Young Irish girls were often forced to peddle their sex to help feed their families.

There was little for the great mass of Irish poor to do but to seek solace together in their isolation and to unite politically, for they realized that in politics numbers count, and this was an asset they possessed. At the turn of the century, poor Irish boys had three options. They could enter the priesthood. If they had large numbers of friends, they could enter politics and utilize their entourage as a political base. (One of the great ward bosses often repeated the Irish battle cry, "The votes, my boy, the votes! That's where they can't stop us, by God. We'll crush them!" And he was right.) And small business was, of course, a possibility if one knew enough neighbors and if one was thrifty and accumulated a bit of capital. Patrick Kennedy took advantage of both the political and the business routes. He saved enough to purchase a tavern that doubled as the local political club, and he cultivated friends, listened to enough complaints of neighbors, and then marshaled this small band of loyal followers for his election to the state legislature. He served five terms and became a state senator.

By 1910 the so-called Irish political machine was systematically organized in almost every ward and operated on the principle of quid pro quo — you scratch my back and I'll scratch yours. Favors were exchanged for favors. When a local boss could deliver several blocks, the residents soon received new streetlights or had the water pipes replaced. A contract for snow removal was usually given to a neighborhood family, and soon it became common knowledge that the votes of several families could mean political jobs and financial security, or a bed in the city hospital for a sick child, or an appointment on the police force.

The electoral basis of American politics prevented the Yankee elite from excluding the Irish. They were forced to accommodate. Patrick Kennedy, Jr., ultimately fell in with another Democratic ward boss, John F. Fitzgerald. "Honey Fitz," as he was affectionately known, was a more established Boston figure than Kennedy. He had spent a year at Harvard College and had worked in the Boston Customs House, where he had made important contacts that became part of his political base. "Honey Fitz" served in the Boston City Council, the State Senate, and the United States House of Representatives. He became one of Boston's most celebrated and colorful mayors — a true character and a notorious practical joker who loved to sing in public. Prohibition was an issue of great interest to him, and his political sophistication is indicated by his motto: "Bigger, better, busier Boston!"

Business and political success raised the Kennedy and Fitzgerald families to the ranks of the middle class, the lace-curtain Irish. Rose Fitzgerald, admitted to Wellesley College, chose instead to attend a private girls' school in France. Kennedy's son Joseph attended the Boston Latin School and Harvard College.

Regardless of their financial success and new-found status, the Kennedys were still excluded from the social circles of Boston's older Brahmin families, whose political morality and transactions were the antithesis of those practiced by the Irish patronage political machine. For Yankees, the purpose of politics was to promote the good life, to moralize men by example, and to enhance their commitment to the Protestant ethic, family, and church. Protestant politicians did not dispense patronage. For them, politics was not a matter of quid pro quo, but rather of political principle. Political questions involved good and evil, right and wrong, not who gets what, where, when, and how. One could not imagine two political styles more diametrically opposed. The conflict between the Protestants and the band of pragmatic, self-serving immigrants who practiced a Robin Hood brand of populist politics could not easily be resolved, but inevitably numbers triumphed, and the Irish made steady inroads on the Boston political scene.

Joseph Kennedy was more sophisticated than his father and more interested in social acceptance. His search for status was rewarded when he became one of the first "outsiders" to be admitted to one of the "right" clubs at Harvard. Some insight into his adult business career and values may be gleaned from an enterprise he undertook while still an undergraduate. During one summer, Kennedy made a substantial amount of money operating a sightseeing bus that went from Boston to Lexington. His management of this small business venture is a classic example of the fusion of capitalism, political influence, and nepotism. The Boston–Lexington route was dominated by the Colonial Auto-Sight-Seeing Company, which paid a three-dollar license fee annually to the city of Boston. When Joseph Kennedy commenced his busing enterprise, the mayor of Boston, Honey Fitz, who happened to be his future father-in-law, suddenly increased the Colonial's fee to $3000 per year, an increase of 1500 percent. The other companies were unable to compete, and young Kennedy soon found himself a monopolist.

Edward Kennedy's father may have learned several lessons from the busing experience — practical lessons that are more valuable than the dicta of business schools. Kennedy Sr. was not to forget the value of contacts, particu-

and selling . . . When the price of a stock was inflated sufficiently, the pool would sell short for huge profits . . . All Kennedy had done, he once said, was to "advertise the stocks." Today such advertising is outlawed.

By the time the market crashed in 1929, Kennedy's personal fortune was estimated at $250 million. In 1980, the Kennedy family fortune is estimated to be in the vicinity of $450 million. Edward Kennedy's annual income from trust funds and stocks is approximately a quarter of a million dollars, and his net worth is estimated to be in the vicinity of $20 million.

In the thirties, Joseph Kennedy may have reminded himself of the lessons learned on warm summer afternoons while driving between Boston and Lexington: Money counts, contacts count, and money and contacts make the world go round. In 1932, in accordance with this principle, he made a very large contribution to the campaign of Franklin Delano Roosevelt, and FDR, himself an advocate of quid pro quo, rewarded him with the chairmanship of the newly created Securities and Exchange Commission. The irony of the appointment greatly amused Wall Street because FDR had given a master manipulator power over a world that is quintessentially manipulative.

Prior to this appointment, Kennedy had established a liquor-importing business, shrewdly anticipating the repeal of Prohibition. The importance of contacts in the liquor business is substantial because of the need for licensing. Kennedy made it a point to become friendly with the President's son, James Roosevelt, and the two utilized their contacts, always operating behind the scenes, to secure the exclusive American franchise for the importation of British whiskeys and gins. The repeal of Prohibition, if nothing else, made them rich.

larly political contacts, once he had realized the po
the state and the salutary effects of nepotism.

After graduation, Joseph Kennedy became a state
examiner, a position that made it possible for hii
gather information on bank mergers. He put the infoi
tion to good use, borrowed money from friends, and c
trolled a bank at the age of twenty-five. He quickly m
tered the complexities of high finance when he becai
assistant general manager of the Quincy Shipyard of tl
Bethlehem Steel Company. He began to speculate in th
market, investing in new businesses, and he specialized ii
companies that were in financial difficulty. He learned
what magnates now know, that the death of one corporation opens the possibility for an inexpensive rebirth and
high profits. In the early twenties, Kennedy was attracted
by the investment possibilities of Hollywood and by its
glamour, and ultimately became board chairman and special advisor to several film and radio companies. He spent
much time in Hollywood, over the objections of his very
devout wife, Rose, and produced several movies. Though he
saw his family infrequently at this time, rumors abounded
in Hollywood that his friendship with the actress Gloria
Swanson was, indeed, close.

Kennedy became a major speculator on Wall Street,
where his activities were shrouded in secrecy. He was a legendary figure on the Street during the Depression, when
millions were losing their life savings and standing in soup
lines. Victor Lasky, a biographer whose antipathy to the
Kennedys is well known in political circles, described Kennedy's activities.

He specialized in setting up pools (along with such partners as
Harry Sinclair and "Sell 'em" Ben Smith), and inflated cheap
stocks through rumors and erratic but well-publicized buying

Kennedy made himself useful to Franklin Roosevelt's cause when he published *I'm for Roosevelt,* a book in which he argued that only Roosevelt would make changes drastic enough to insure the viability of the capitalist system. It was a shrewd observation, for FDR did just that, and he did it against the militant opposition of businessmen.

Joseph Kennedy was not one to write hagiographic tracts without expecting something in return. He was rewarded in 1938, when the President appointed him ambassador to the Court of St. James. The irony of the grandson of an Irish-Catholic immigrant's representing Protestant America before the Anglican throne did not escape him. For years rumors had circulated in Washington that Kennedy had presidential aspirations. His hopes, however, were dashed in 1940, when FDR, concerned by Kennedy's political ambitions, eased him out of the administration. Kennedy infuriated the British while he was ambassador by voicing the opinion that the Germans would probably win the war and that the United States, therefore, should arrange a favorable accommodation with Hitler. He is also reported to have argued that Jews should fight their own battles in Europe, as the Irish had done years before. He failed to grasp the meaning of fascism and nazism, seemed vaguely sympathetic toward some of Hitler's aims, and always considered communism a far greater threat to the capitalist system than nazism. It is not surprising that Joseph McCarthy was a frequent guest at the Kennedy compound in the early fifties and was reported to have exchanged political favors with young John Kennedy while the latter was in Congress. Robert Kennedy later became a member of the McCarthy investigation subcommittee staff.

The Kennedy boys went to old New England prep schools and Harvard College. The girls, however, went to parochial schools and Catholic women's colleges. Joseph Kennedy may have transcended the limitations of his youth, but he was surely a product of Irish culture, which was then still sexist enough that men and not women were expected to achieve and that it fostered aggressiveness in men and passivity in women.

Although Joseph Kennedy made millions, he cultivated a disdain for business among his sons. He often described that world as "full of knaves and fools." He made it perfectly clear that the Kennedy boys were financially secure and need not pursue careers in business. The fundamental lesson that Joseph Kennedy taught his children, the sine qua non of his world view, was that winning was critical.

Joseph Kennedy liked the sound of the "family motto" and repeated it forcefully to his children: "We don't want any losers around here. In this family we want winners!" Kennedy advocated a view of the world that was a fusion of Machiavelli and Horatio Alger, a philosophy steeped in the ethic that ends justify means, and that power and public service are the proper goals. For Rose Kennedy, religiosity may have been a prime virtue. For her husband and sons, however, the force of will and the attainment of power were the ultimate.

Families often create legends around their eldest son. The Kennedys portrayed Joseph Jr. as his father's most adept student, the dominant and eldest brother who challenged and defeated his siblings to remain *primus inter pares*. He was to die in the service of his country during World War II.

The second son, John Fitzgerald Kennedy, was more aloof and intellectual than his grandfathers, but, like them, he was proficient in the practice of artful compromise and realized the need for moderating principles in the service of ambition. John Kennedy evoked a charisma and mystique that, coupled with a disciplined and affluent campaign organization, permitted him to become the first Roman Catholic to occupy the White House. When he first ran for the U.S. House of Representatives, his father pulled every political string at his disposal to help. But ultimately, to the Kennedys, winning in Massachusetts would be considered a modest victory. The power and the glory of the family could never adequately be tested in that state alone — the stakes were too small. The national electorate and the White House would prove a more worthy challenge.

But the power of the presidency was not enough for this family. Once elected, Kennedy appointed his brother attorney general of the United States. The appointment of Robert Kennedy, a former aide to Senator Joseph McCarthy and a man whose judicial and legislative experience was minimal, evoked a storm of protest from the more liberal members of the bar and the bench.

The third son, Edward Kennedy, remained in Massachusetts and waited, but not for long. The President's seat in the U.S. Senate had become vacant, and he persuaded the governor of Massachusetts to appoint one Benjamin Smith II, an obscure citizen of the Bay State who had been the President's roommate at Harvard, to fill the vacancy. This tactic was designed to make the seat "safe" by placing it in the hands of an unambitious friend who would gladly step aside when Edward Kennedy became old enough to run in 1962.

Smith's elevation was viewed by some as an outrageous display of nepotism. To others, it was simply a matter of *realpolitik*. But to the Kennedys it was an obvious and necessary step in dynastic ambition that Joseph Kennedy would have seen as part of the normal course of business.

2

Kennedy Campaigning, 1962

EDWARD KENNEDY announced his senatorial candidacy on schedule and without embarrassment, although he could not cite, in his defense, a lengthy and substantial record of political and legal accomplishments. All he had done was to manage his brother's presidential campaign in some Western states and then serve as a dollar-a-year assistant district attorney in Suffolk County, Massachusetts. Some good citizens of the Bay State were outraged. One of the commonwealth's moral overseers, an eminent Boston Brahmin, Professor Mark DeWolfe Howe of the Harvard Law School, denounced Edward Kennedy's candidacy on television as "preposterous and outrageous." Howe, a supporter of Kennedy's opponent, Edward McCormack, stated what some believe are facts and others believe is bias. "On any achievement of his own, Ted Kennedy, at the age of thirty, is not qualified to seek such a high office . . . I cannot believe that were his name not Kennedy, or his brother not in the White House, and perhaps also his other brother not in the Department of Justice, that he could under any circumstances have put himself forward as a candidate for the United States Senate."

For PR men the election was a dream. The brother of the President of the United States, thirty years old, with no qualifications, was seeking his brother's seat. Everybody knew he was a candidate only because his brother was the President. To the sensitive, it was an affront. To the political, it was an inevitability. Edward McCormack, Kennedy's adversary for the Democratic nomination, was himself a member of a minidynasty, a petty fiefdom, as it were, for his uncle was John McCormack, the Speaker of the U.S. House of Representatives. Kennedy and McCormack were opposed by H. Stuart Hughes, a distinguished European historian at Harvard and nephew of former Chief Justice Charles Evans Hughes. For comic relief, the Republicans had a dynastic junior in George Lodge, son of Senator Henry Cabot Lodge and grandson of the venerable Senator Lodge who had blocked Woodrow Wilson's proposal for the League of Nations. The media loved it. The prospect of a younger brother embarrassing the President, and the prospect of ancient John McCormack racked with anger, blocking presidential legislation, amused the national press.

The critical test for Edward Kennedy took place when the candidates confronted each other in a series of televised debates. Kennedy was the youngest, least educated, and certainly least sophisticated participant, so the family prevailed on wiser heads. A Harvard professor of government and leading Massachusetts liberal tutored Edward Kennedy, plied him with facts and figures, names and dates, trends and countertrends: the gross national product of France, current mortgage rates in Peoria, the military budget of Russia. The Kennedys had grasped that a flood of facts and figures, a barrage of statistics, contain a latent and unspoken message: The candidate who can cite hundreds of figures must be not only highly intelligent and educated, but also a man who cares, for he would not have mastered these data if he were not interested in using them to benefit the public. The medium is the message.

The Kennedy rhetoric is staccato, pulsating in its beat. The impression is that of a drum being constantly beaten. The pulse and the beat, the emphasis on the word "I," convey the message that the speaker is quick and tough, stern and in command. Kennedy is now so well trained, after seventeen years in American politics, that he cannot give a speech without providing a cascade of facts, figures, data, and trends. It is as if the outpouring of facts negates the need for argument. The facts speak for themselves. The facts are the speech. The factual speaker need not be a master of logic, a thoughtful man of argument, he need have only a good memory, the capability to be preprogrammed. Kennedy's impromptu presentations are often chaotic and ungrammatical, though programmatic and stilted. Their cadence is that of a man who is carefully rehearsed, but who worries that unless he rushes through his part, his spontaneous and fragmented true self will intrude and muddy the act.

Edward Kennedy's first campaign offers many examples of the impromptu and the preprogrammed style. Both are designed to overwhelm the listener with names, dates, facts, references to extensive travel and visits, interviews both with famous people and common men in all walks of life, changes in the price of commodities, references to constant study of a large variety of problems — problems international in scale and problems in a town in Wisconsin. In 1962 Kennedy campaigned on the slogan, "He can do more for Massachusetts," an obvious, but unspoken, reference to the fact that he was the brother of the President, and his supporters claimed that "He speaks with a voice that will be heard." A sophisticated reporter, who obviously understood the nepotistic character of the slogans, asked, nevertheless, what Kennedy meant when he said that he spoke "with a voice that will be heard." Kennedy's answer is a classic example of his speaking style.

> I was the campaign manager for my brother in 1958. I traveled throughout this state. I've talked with the fishermen about the problems in Gloucester. I've talked to the shoe and leather people who have worked in the factories in Lynn and Lowell . . . I believe as well that a United States senator is going to vote on matters not only of particular and peculiar importance to Massachusetts, but also to the problems that we face as a nation. I spent three months in Wisconsin and have talked to the dairy farmers. You pay twenty-seven cents for a quart of milk and the dairy farmer receives five cents; and yet his income has been declining in recent years. We as senators from Massachusetts are going to be voting on this matter. I spent three months in West Virginia, and talked to the coal miners of West Virginia, and have seen what happens when automation happens in these coal fields, and I have spent some time and continuing study in the other parts of the countries throughout the world . . . — how our taxpayers' dollars are going to be spent . . . are we going to support the Upper Volta project in Ghana . . . are we going to certainly support the regimes of Mr. Sekou Touré in Guinea.

In two or three minutes, Kennedy managed to refer to Massachusetts, Gloucester, Lynn, Lowell, the United States, Wisconsin, West Virginia, Ghana, and Guinea. He referred to the fact that he spoke to fishermen, shoe and leather people, coal miners, and Sekou Touré. He also managed to note the retail price of milk in Wisconsin and the amount received by the dairy farmer. It may be too much to expect candidates to discuss cause and effect, to place facts within a meaningful framework or propose solutions to some problems in a half-hour television debate, but there are few instances in the entire 1962 campaign when Kennedy made a serious effort to put his names, dates, and facts into significant and related patterns.

Eighteen years later, Kennedy's impromptu speeches are a bit smoother and more reasoned and he is capable, at times, of pursuing an argument to its conclusion. However, the old Kennedy lives, the preprogrammed Kennedy, the Kennedy of the stilted formulaic rhetoric, the Kennedy of the bombastic delivery, and the Kennedy who name-drops. The old style was very visible in an interview with the *New York Times*, published on January 10, 1980. Kennedy answered questions with an endless series of facts, a staccato tempo, evasive answers, formulaic rhetoric, and a linear presentation of relevant arguments. When asked what he believed the nation needs in a President for the eighties, Kennedy replied, facts in hand, ". . . we appeared to be really lurching from crisis to crisis in domestic affairs and in foreign affairs: that we saw our rates of inflation growing from less than 5 percent to over 12 or 12½ percent, interest rates climbing from 6 percent to some 15 percent; the value of gold going right up through the roof." Part of his answer illustrates the rhythmic tempo, the beat of a man who can do things.

The evasive answer remains central to his repertoire. When asked, for the first of three times, about the relevance of his personal behavior with specific reference to Chappaquiddick, to womanizing, and to drinking heavily, Kennedy responded in part, "I have always felt that this campaign would be decided by the type of direction that we could offer — that I could offer to the country during the course of this campaign — how I approach the central issues . . ." When asked a second time about Chappaquid-

dick, Kennedy responded that if there were facts that con-
travened his testimony, he would not run for the presidency. When asked a third time about his private life,
Kennedy answered by utilizing the dual tactic of evasion
and a barrage of facts. Question: "As far as the other issues
in your private life, is there anything you think that you
can say or do to put an end to the recurring reports about
them, or do you feel that will continue?" Answer: "No, I
think that the American people want a discussion; they
want debate on the central issues of our time. I think working people are concerned about the fact that their wages
are held to 7 percent and the prices are going up to 13 percent . . ." When asked, "What's the lesson of Iran and
Afghanistan for the United States?" Kennedy's answer
was, "Well, I think that American foreign policy has to be a
foreign policy that, one, is certain, two, is predictable, and
three, is sounded with one voice, not a number of voices
. . ." Is there a serious policy maker in Washington who
could possibly disagree with these platitudes?

Kennedy has, however, substantially matured in the past
eighteen years. Though the formulaic and evasive answer
reappears, Kennedy has worked hard and been receptive to
new ideas during his seventeen years in the Senate, and he
is now familiar with major aspects of public policy and international relations. His knowledge is substantial, although he and his staff have created rather neat categories
into which fact and theory are stored until supporting evidence is needed. The Kennedy presentation usually seems
to have been "canned." This may be the price that must
be paid for having so extensive a staff.

When Kennedy ran for the Senate in 1962, a few months
after his thirtieth birthday, he was without substantial
achievement. In fact, the most publicized act of his adult

years was his expulsion from Harvard for cheating. In America it is considered necessary, when running for the Senate, to display what are commonly known as "accomplishments." These were "provided" for Kennedy and presented to the Massachusetts public in a brochure — an interesting artifact — a construction not precisely fictitious, but nevertheless not material. A very attractive tricolored campaign brochure was printed and distributed throughout the state, depicting Kennedy as a man of substance, a man with a long history of what was called "community service." The message was simple: Kennedy was an elder statesman of Boston philanthropy. The brochure noted that he had been selected as one of the ten outstanding men of the year by the Boston Junior Chamber of Commerce, that he had received the Order of Merit of the Republic of Italy for his interest and achievements on behalf of Italian culture and progress. His work as chairman of a successful American Cancer Society campaign was noted, as was the fact that Edward Kennedy had been chairman of the United Fund Health and Fitness Fair. The brochure listed additional associations: trustee and member of the executive board, Massachusetts Chapter, Arthritis and Rheumatism Foundation; Judge Advocate of the Polish-American Veterans Post of Boston; member of the advisory board, Emmanuel College; and finally, president of the Joseph P. Kennedy, Jr. Foundation.

The brochure was designed to meet a serious problem. Kennedy, in fact, had almost no political experience and it was necessary to create for him the image of a legitimate and mature senatorial candidate. Kennedy had been neither a congressman, mayor, state senator, attorney general, nor anything else, and that is why the brochure is interesting. The achievements noted are not those customarily associated with a senatorial candidate from a major state, but they are "accomplishments" of a sort, accomplishments that lend not only a patina of public service to a candidate, but public service that is cued into causes that are politically exploitable. The brochure connects Kennedy to "motherhood and God." He is saluted by Italy and has served Poland, nations that have supplied Massachusetts with large numbers of voters. He fights cancer, arthritis, and rheumatism, diseases from which large numbers of Massachusetts constituents probably suffer. And, like most senatorial candidates, he served on the board of a college and a foundation, even though the foundation is one of his family's making.

Although Kennedy did not have a substantial record, he had the capacity to campaign fifteen to twenty hours a day. Neither he nor his brothers forgot the Algerisms that Joseph Kennedy had taught them. But in Edward Kennedy's case, an exhausting campaign was necessary for two reasons. The tireless candidate is a candidate who not only contacts large numbers of delegates and voters, but also emits the latent message that he is a serious candidate, a dedicated candidate, and a candidate, who if elected, will serve the public as a tireless agent.

The pressure was on. Edward Kennedy had to win the Senate election. The embarrassment that the President might suffer if his brother lost would be politically most disadvantageous. The Kennedys would not look foolish, but the political judgment of the President would be called into question. Edward Kennedy did not disappoint his brother. He campaigned at a tempo so fierce that McCormack's aides could hardly believe it. One of them commented on his activity: "I don't say he's been in every town, but I guarantee that he's been in 75 to 80 percent of the towns and cities of Massachusetts. He's been in places like . . . Gill, who ever goes to Gill? This guy went to Gill to see one delegate they've got there. Most people wouldn't know where Gill was . . . You know where Gill is? . . . Well, Ted Kennedy has been to Gill."

This kind of doggedness, plus a campaign organization of unprecedented size and financial resources, produced a landslide victory. The effort in 1980 will be organized along the model campaign of 1962. The men who ran the organization then were largely professionals who had managed the campaign of John Kennedy in 1960, and the sheer size of the campaign was something that the citizens of Massachusetts had never seen before. The Kennedys purchased more television and radio time and exhibited more minutes of documentary films and video tape on television than all the other candidates combined. They purchased time on nine television stations, including stations in the states of New York and Rhode Island, and with rare exception it was prime time. They bought time on more than fifty English-language radio stations and more than twenty foreign-language radio stations. They purchased prime billboard space throughout the commonwealth. They provided automobiles on election day throughout the state to drive voters to the polls. They employed the services of a highly reputable public-opinion firm, which took samples before the convention and at several points during the campaign. For people in local communities who wished to open a Kennedy campaign headquarters, the staff provided typewriters, telephones, water coolers, signs, electricity, janitorial service, insurance, and office furniture.

The size of the campaign is indicated by the fact that Kennedy's organization distributed at least 500,000 bumper stickers, made 300,000 telephone calls, received at least 200,000 written letters of support, and posted more than a million pieces of mail. Envelopes and letterheads were printed in three colors, expensive though that may be, and Kennedy's advertising agency arranged for the publication of an eight-page rotogravure handout printed in two colors and entitled *The Ted Kennedy Story*.

The effort by no means stopped here. Roughly 160,000 citizens of Massachusetts who were not registered to vote were contacted through the mail by means of a printed postcard; Kennedy's aides estimate that they registered approximately 25,000 people. Special project groups were created to work with labor, the elderly, Jews, and a variety of ethnic and religious groups. Special mailings were prepared for each group, and minicampaign organizations were set up, based on religious membership and ethnic origin. The extent of the division of labor of the Kennedy campaign organization was unprecedented. Area coordinators were recruited from every senatorial district, and leaders for every major city, virtually every ward, and thousands of precincts. In some large cities where streets run for miles, block leaders were enlisted to contact voters in individual apartment houses and housing projects, block by block. Several syndicated columnists and Washington correspondents described the Kennedy effort as the most thorough statewide campaign they had ever witnessed.

Candidates in Massachusetts are required to report their campaign expenditures. Edward Kennedy's treasurer reported expenditures of $421,442. Given the extent of the campaign — the fact that Kennedy had more television time and documentary films and newspaper advertising than all of his rivals combined — the efficiency of the Kennedy operation, dollar for dollar, is astounding. The senior author of this book and a large staff analyzed the 1962 campaign (*Kennedy Campaigning: The System and Style as Practiced by Edward Kennedy*). We made meticulous and conservative estimates of nine major Kennedy expenditures: television and radio, newspaper advertising, postage, billboards, stationery, tabloid, bumper stickers, public-opinion polls, and rent for headquarters. We concluded that these alone came to a cost of $422,255. It was impossible to determine the cost of many other items, both large (documentary films) and small (straw hats).

Many of these costs are public knowledge. Information about television and radio time are available at the studio, and newspaper rates are available for the asking. Advertising agencies reported to us the cost of billboards, and our staff toured the state to estimate the number Kennedy purchased. Distributors provided us with the cost of buttons, streamers, novelties, and so forth, and PR men estimated the cost of brochures. But much of the information was supplied by Kennedy aides who were interviewed.

Massachusetts is a state composed of ethnic groups that still maintain relatively separate identities. Everyone who campaigns for major office in the commonwealth establishes campaign headquarters in Italian areas, Polish areas, Irish areas, and so on. But the Kennedys operate on a grander scale. With full knowledge that ethnic groups would play a significant role in a future campaign, Edward Kennedy toured Italy, Ireland, and Israel in 1961. Men of power are always accompanied by cameramen, and Kennedy was not an exception. A film of his trip to Italy was made and the way that film was used during the campaign was described by one Kennedy campaign chieftain.

A film was made in Italy showing his trip there — everything from giving pennies to Italian children in the street to an audience with the Pope — which was then distributed to Italian clubs for showing all over the state. You would just call and say the club in such and such an area would like to see a film and a man would come down with a projector and the film, the works, to show it to the club. To do this on a large scale costs tremendous amounts of money. But this is what was done.

According to a Kennedy aide who is now managing the state of New York for Kennedy in 1980, the organization in 1962 had six major tasks: the recruitment of senatorial city, town, ward, and precinct coordinators and volunteer workers; a signature drive for pledges of support designed to give signers a sense of belonging and the Kennedys an opportunity to recruit volunteers; a registration drive to enroll new voters — particularly young ones who were pro-Kennedy; mailings aimed at advertising the candidate and maintaining good will; the creation of special project task forces to organize ethnic, religious, and occupational groups; and a telephone campaign to reach possible stragglers. This is the traditional Kennedy campaign division of labor.

The tasks are so extensive and costly that only candidates with a very superior staff, dozens of media specialists, coordinators of quality, and very substantial financial resources could execute the plan within one large industrial state, let alone the United States. The ability of Kennedy to campaign in his past style and that of his brothers will be severely curtailed by the new federal law that regulates spending in presidential primaries and general elections, assuming that he and other candidates obey the law. Three years after his election, Carter is still being investigated by the Federal Elections Commission.

For presidential candidates who accept matching funds, the total amount that may be spent by one candidate in all primaries is $15.9 million in the 1980 campaign. The amounts that may be spent in particular states are also stipulated — for example, $2.9 million in New York, $3.4 million in California, and $890,000 in Massachusetts. This means that candidates must pick and choose states with care so that they have enough money to launch an all-out effort and spend the maximum amount at a critical point in the campaign. This could alter Kennedy's strategy — for example if, in May, Kennedy is far behind, he could decide that Carter must be beaten in New York or Pennsylvania. If he had spent the bulk of his $15.9 million by May or June, he could not make a major effort. If the law were not operative and Kennedy had not accepted matching funds, he probably could raise large sums in these states.

He could even be damaged by the law that regulates how a candidate qualifies for matching. To qualify, a candidate must raise at least $5000 in each of twenty states in contributions of $250 or less. Kennedy, Brown, and Carter qualified for, and accepted, dollar-for-dollar matching funds. Individuals may not contribute in excess of $25,000 to a candidate or a committee. The law was designed to lessen sharply the influence of "fat cats." This limit probably hurts Republicans more than Democrats; John Connally, for example, who has very large sums available, refused matching grants.

The long-term significance of the law, despite its egalitarian intent, will probably be to strengthen the role of institutionalized special interests, corporations, and political-action committees, because executives may contribute to them without limit. The net effect of the law in 1980 will be disadvantageous to Kennedy because it limits the size of the Kennedy operation by placing a ceiling on expenditures and curbing large contributors.

The Kennedy organization may define their objectives

and create a division of labor in 1980 that is modeled on that of 1960 and 1962, but the limits on campaign spending will require that some objectives be abandoned and others curtailed. The cost of a full national effort in the Kennedy grand manner would be beyond the law. But the men who run the campaign in 1980 should be in a good position to make judicious cuts because many of them were involved in the 1962 effort.

The Kennedy organization, large as it is, has always been a family enterprise. In 1962, the organization in Massachusetts was headed by a brother-in-law, Stephen Smith, who now heads the national campaign. The sense of a family affair is reinforced by the fact that cousins and many close friends from 1962 surround Stephen Smith. To anticipate what they are likely to do in Kennedy's drive for the presidency, the dynamics of the first campaign are relevant.

In a search for delegates in 1962, Stephen Smith set up a control system that would make it possible for him to know at all times who was committed to Kennedy and who to McCormack, and who was undecided. This, in itself, is not the most arduous of tasks. However, Smith gathered thousands of bits of data concerning the public and private life of delegates, data that could be used for purposes of persuasion or condemnation. The effort required a large-scale information-gathering network, a network patterned after that which President Kennedy used in 1960.

The data on delegates were not punched on IBM cards or processed by a computer. Stephen Smith was apparently so familiar with them that he could match an undecided or pro-McCormack delegate with the Kennedy agent most likely to have something in common with him. One of the more amusing bits of political maneuvering during the campaign concerned the Little League. A Kennedy campaign manager reported the following story:

> We find out, for example that Joe Jones from Quincy, is very active in Little League, and we find . . . two or three people very close to Quincy . . . who are with Kennedy. We send one of these people down. They start out on a mutual level of Little League and they talk and they become friends . . .
> There's a fellow in one of the southern towns who . . . thought that he had played baseball with one of Ted Kennedy's roommates. A contact was made. So is there any friendship and he says ya, fine . . . You find . . . a delegate from, say, Marlboro undecided, but he's always taking a cue from . . . some fellow in Framingham . . . So when this is noted on a card, you talk to the guy from Framingham, . . . tell him that Ted Kennedy's good for the party, . . . then find out if he belongs to a labor union and what type of work he does. So Ted does see him and talks with him and they talk baseball and they talk football and they talk . . . It's really a selling problem . . .

In order to sell Edward Kennedy to the people of Massachusetts in 1962, Kennedy aides evolved a presentation that appealed specifically to ethnic groups and particular cities and towns. Every speech was custom-made.

When visiting cities in Massachusetts, Kennedy spoke on one or two matters that were of special concern to local inhabitants. Advance men on his staff toured the state and carefully prepared analyses of local problems. In New Bedford, where fishing is an important industry, Kennedy stated that existing federal subsidies for fishing boat construction should be broadened by legislation he would introduce if elected. He also promised that he would seek ways of getting the Food and Drug Administration to approve fish flour for certain purposes, and that he would try to secure federal support for highway construction in the New Bedford area.

The meticulous attention to detail that typified the work of Kennedy's advance men was clear at the Blessed Sacrament Feast in New Bedford, one of the largest Portuguese religious functions in the United States. Kennedy, the featured speaker, praised the indomitable Portuguese explorers of the golden age of Lusitania. "We are fortunate," he remarked, "to have here in Massachusetts more Americans of Portuguese descent than in any other state in the Union. Portugal is one of our oldest allies. Portugal stands firmly against Communism, even to the point of allowing our country to use, free of charge, the Azores base, which is the most important air base in the Atlantic Ocean." Kennedy then criticized the Walter-McCarran Immigration Act, which limits Portuguese immigration. The statute, he noted, is "injuring our nation by depriving us of the historical source of strength and growth."

The basic Kennedy speech is like a jigsaw puzzle, the pieces of which are put together in infinite combinations. In Fall River, a city in which the French-speaking population is large, Edward Kennedy spoke of the glories of French culture and French politics, the tradition of liberty, and the invention of natural rights. In Brookline, an affluent and largely Jewish suburb of Boston, Edward Kennedy naturally emphasized the need to defend Israel. No local nuance was neglected by the candidate. While addressing a large crowd in the Italo-American section of Boston, his opening words were spoken in Italian. The *Boston Globe*, much bemused, reported that, ". . . the dialect wasn't discernible — nor for that matter was his message — but it was in Italian and it went over big."

No Kennedy campaign is complete without pollsters and data. The Kennedys hired the best and used their data with skill. When the pollsters found that Kennedy was a good deal more popular with female voters than with males, Kennedy began to spend more time before women's groups, and his mother and wife were used more often to make spot appearances. *Coffee with the Candidate*, a documentary for television, starring Edward and his wife and mother, was aired during the morning so that housewives, while they did their housework, would have an opportunity to see the family.

Housework may be tedious and daily life dull, but compensations exist. Through reverie and dream, fantasy and projection, it is possible to identify with the heroes of the age and find excitement and glamour. American boys "become" Babe Ruth and American girls "become" Jackie Kennedy. To some, the Kennedys are aggressive and "Irish." To others, they are a First Family. Today, Ted Kennedy is still the beneficiary of the image of power, affluence, and chic that, for so many, epitomizes "the American Dream."

3

Seventeen Years in the Senate

THE FORECASTS from Washington on the 1980 presidential elections are divided and bitter. Edward Kennedy is either heralded as the only candidate who can lead the nation or condemned as an opportunist who would lead it right down the road to ruin. His seventeen years in the Senate are evidence to some that he was a daring and progressive activist, but to others his record demonstrates that although he may attract glamorous media exposure with the Kennedy name, he accomplishes very little of substance. On the one hand, he is perceived as an outstanding administrator, a crafty investigator, and a commanding floor leader, but on the other he is seen as the beneficiary of the Kennedy mystique and the creation of a prodigious staff, a staff that only Kennedy money could buy. He is called a quintessential "liberal," yet his most notable victories in the Senate have been scored on such "conservative" legislation as the deregulation of the airlines, a drug industry reform bill that favored the big American drug companies, and an attempted revision of the U.S. criminal code.

Consumer activist Ralph Nader, for one, is undecided

about Kennedy. He views Jimmy Carter as "a Republican in Democrat clothing," and voices strong approval of Kennedy as a senator, saying that his voting record "on bills considered important by consumer, environmental, and tax reform groups has been among the best in the Senate." Nader, however, castigates Kennedy for weakening his own most important and progressive bills dealing with national health insurance, corporate mergers, and drug industry reform. Referring to Kennedy's penchant for compromise by quid pro quo, Nader remarked, "This is his way of distinguishing between modest compromise and immodest abdication in the legislative and political process."

An assistant secretary in the Carter administration evaluated Kennedy and his career differently: "He doesn't really possess any great abilities, he's not all that bright, and his legislative record isn't very good. He hasn't even gotten his pet project, the health insurance bill, out of committee yet. But he does have the capacity to lead because he's a good communicator, which no president since his brother has been. He can mobilize public opinion, elicit an enormous amount of work from a topnotch staff, and he can make decisions."

Syndicated columnist Jack Anderson, on the other hand, believes that Kennedy is a bright and able politician and cites Kennedy's performance during committee hearings as evidence. When Kennedy's subcommittee held hearings on the ITT involvement in Chile, for example, Anderson said that on several occasions he thought Kennedy had missed obvious opportunities to catch a witness contradicting himself. In retrospect, though, he realized that Kennedy was actually waiting for just the right moment to catch the witness off guard. The senator would continue to probe patiently until the witness made himself vulnerable and then spring the critical questions.

Anderson, like many Washington correspondents, is impressed with Kennedy's performance in committee but skeptical of his personality. He has commented: "There must be a major flaw in his character, because of the cheating in school, the speeding incident, the socializing, and the blatant dishonesty about Chappaquiddick. When faced with facts, he still retrenches and refuses to answer questions openly. Whether or not that would affect his national leadership ability is another question."

Everyone seems to have lingering questions and major reservations about Kennedy. There is a sense of hesitancy concerning his politics, his positions on critical issues, and his personal life. He is the object of fierce devotion, rabid hatred, or a complicated love-hate-love mentality, and he is rarely discussed with nonchalance. Almost everyone, nevertheless, acknowledges that he is an astute and diligent senator, that he has assembled the best staff on Capitol Hill, and that, more often than not, he can get things done.

There were several long years of apprenticeship in the Senate before Kennedy developed legislative expertise, and his liberalism was largely the product of the tumultuous sixties and of family indoctrination. As the youngest child in a very aggressive family, he was often the pawn of elder siblings and was raised in the frequent company of world leaders. He learned at an early age that it was necessary to be good-natured, accommodating, and aggressive in order to survive, assets that proved to be equally crucial for ascension in the ranks of the U.S. Senate. Kennedy time and again illustrated his instincts for survival while making use of the family charm.

When he entered the Senate in 1962, his first act was to pay his respects to the elder powers of the Senate. He joked with the aged Richard Russell of Georgia about the fact that both of them had been the youngest men in the Senate, Russell in 1932 and Kennedy thirty years later. Russell chided him with "That's true, son, but I had already been governor of my state by then!" When he approached the conservative southern demagogue, James Eastland of Mississippi, he was welcomed with postbreakfast shots of bourbon, and from that time onward, the two became close colleagues as the young Kennedy served under Eastland for years on the Judiciary Committee.

During his first two years in the Senate, Kennedy was careful not to take his relationship with his brother John, then President, for granted or to curry his favor. He meticulously observed Senate protocol, remained unobtrusive, and played the role of a passive and obedient freshman. He carefully learned the rules of the upper chamber and the customs of his seniors, since apprentices were expected to master innumerable lessons, rules, and traditions of the "club," making sure, for example, that the tone during a debate was always civil and that debate was reciprocal. No member was to be neglected or offended because this might lead him to monopolize Senate debate through the filibuster. When engaged in committee business, those senators who would be directly affected by a bill were to be informed of its progress. Eventually juniors such as Kennedy would learn to swap favors for key votes and bring pressure to bear on recalcitrant members. Ultimately a newcomer's power and prestige might become great enough to command the attention of the media and mold public opinion to further his aims. This skill came easily to the youngest Kennedy.

Fifteen months after entering the Senate, Kennedy delivered his maiden speech on the floor. He prefaced it with an apology for his premature oration, saying, "It is with some hesitation that I rise to speak on the pending legislation before the Senate. A freshman Senator should be seen, not heard; should learn, not teach." But, he insisted, he felt compelled to speak his mind on the landmark civil rights bill before the Congress, particularly because "my brother was the first President of the United States to state publicly that segregation is morally wrong. His heart and soul are in this bill." After a moving speech on the urgency of civil rights reform, he resumed his back row seat in the Senate and continued to defer to his elders.

Kennedy was warmly accepted by his colleagues, largely because he was polite, law-abiding, and deferential. Unlike many young senators, he postponed the pursuit of publicity and a reputation as a "national senator." He served as quietly as a Kennedy could during his early years in the Senate and gradually rose in the power structure by accepting posts and immersing himself in the work of various subcommittees. In 1965 Eastland made him the chairman of the Subcommittee on Refugees, and in that capacity he undertook the first of several trips to Vietnam to inspect refugee camps there. He voiced support for U.S. policies in Vietnam while his brother was President and for several years after his death, and only later began to shift publicly on the issue, in 1967. At that time his older brother Bobby was making his name as one of the chief spokesmen against the war, so Ted deferred to him and risked only veiled, low-key criticisms of U.S. policies from his position on the Refugees Subcommittee. After a second trip to Saigon and the camps in 1968, he spoke with fervor about the damage that the war was causing to the people and culture of Indochina.

Historians have advanced numerous theories about Ted Kennedy's late reversal on the war in Vietnam. Biographer Robert Sherrill maintained that Kennedy's opposition to the war was weak, predicated largely on his interest in the refugees and on the economic inefficiency of the war rather than on the ultimate moral question of the killing of Vietnamese people: "The war, to him, was not wrong because it was just plain wrong, not wrong because the United States had dreadfully interfered with another country's private affairs, not wrong because Americans were being forced to die for Ky and Thieu, but rather because it had become too costly, because the war's books weren't balancing." Other biographers have argued that Ted deferred to his brother Robert on the war for two reasons. RFK, as the oldest surviving Kennedy brother, was given the right to lead the family on a crucial issue, and his career came before that of the younger brother. And second, the family in concert determined that it would be counterproductive for both of the two surviving brothers of John Kennedy to attack the administration policies continued by Kennedy's successor, Lyndon Johnson. According to this interpretation, Ted Kennedy's silence on the war could again be viewed as political rather than moral. His eventual emergence in 1968 as an opponent of the war, with Richard Nixon in office and his second brother dead, could demonstrate either a belated recognition of the moral position on the Vietnam War, or it may have been the first time that he was free to voice his true feelings.

Kennedy's first congressional battle was to uphold the civil rights issues that he inherited from his brother John. As a member of the Judiciary Committee, Kennedy was assigned to the Subcommittee on Constitutional Rights, and from that post he sponsored an amendment to the Civil Rights Act of 1965 that would ban the use of literacy tests and poll taxes as qualifications for voters, both of which discriminated mainly against poor and black voters. He won much praise in and out of Congress and fought persistently for his amendment, which was narrowly defeated in a Senate vote. That same year he successfully steered through the Senate the Johnson administration's Immigration and Nationality Act, which eliminated national origins quotas from the immigration laws.

But Kennedy was sharply criticized soon after his Senate victory when he proposed that a family friend, Boston Municipal Judge Francis Morrissey, be named to a federal judgeship. Since his father demanded the nomination, presumably to pay off political favors, Ted stood behind Morrissey even when committee members accused his candidate of having shady connections and of being unqualified for the job. Kennedy was damaged by this but refused to yield, presumably for reasons of family loyalty.

Ted was also criticized for voting with Republicans and several other Democrats (including brother Bobby) to allow the big drug companies to keep patents on newly discovered products funded by the government, presumably because he was under heavy pressure from the industry lobbyists. Russell Long of Louisiana authored the amendment that would allow the government to keep these patents, and Kennedy voted against him. He would again be accused, almost fifteen years later, of bowing to pressure from the drug companies and greatly modifying his own bill to reform the drug industry.

In 1966, students in his own home state of Massachusetts, like those on every major campus in the country, began to protest induction into the army. Kennedy proposed a major change in the draft law that year, favoring a national lottery within a concept that seemed almost radical at the time. He advanced a broad plan for comprehensive and universal national service, which did not prove to be particularly popular with the youth constituency in Massachusetts. He proposed to terminate deferments for students and establish uniform standards for induction, arguing that the draft laws discriminated heavily against the poor and black segments of the population. But at the same time, he opposed the creation of an all-volunteer army because it might conceivably become an all-poor-black and -minority organization, and thus be even more inequitable than the current system. It was a coherent and progressive policy that undercut charges by critics that he tended to pander to the youth constituency in the country. But the program as a whole was too radical for the Senate, and Kennedy's proposals were defeated. Several years later, in 1969, President Nixon instituted his own national lottery, partly to quell student uprisings around the country, and was accused of "stealing" the issue from Kennedy.

As early as 1966, Kennedy became more firmly identified with topical liberal causes. In addition to his support of civil rights, he suggested that more funds be diverted to social programs, particularly in health and education. He advanced legislation that would send teachers to deprived areas and a bill that would establish neighborhood health centers in needy communities; both of the proposals were adopted. He demonstrated his growing strength in the Senate in 1967 when he successfully led the attack against a bill that would have delayed enforcement of the Supreme Court's one-man, one-vote decision.

Yet his own power base began to give way after an important political victory in 1969, and he was wholly responsible for his later decline in the Senate leadership structure. In January of that year he opposed the conservative southern strongman, Russell Long of Louisiana, chairman of the powerful Senate Finance Committee, for the position of majority whip, which Long had held for years. After intense lobbying among his Senate colleagues and a bitter intra-Senate campaign, Kennedy unseated Long by a vote of 31 to 26. At this point Kennedy was on his way to becoming a "national senator" who was capable of securing a base for the 1972 presidential campaign. Sherrill maintained that Kennedy's triumph was not significant, ". . . seeing as how Long was not only sloppy in his administration of the job but was best known as the Senate's resident drunk."

Kennedy began to advocate strongly the programs associated with the liberal wing of the Democratic party, particularly those of Hubert Humphrey. He developed a deep desire to prevent Nixon from negating the policies inspired by his brothers, but soon came to realize that as majority whip he could do little to advance liberal causes. A majority whip is expected to serve his fellow senators, performing such chores as scheduling members' time on the floor, keeping track of their pet programs and bills, notifying them in offices and committee meetings when they have to appear on the floor to vote, and helping them to secure whatever favors they might need.

For several months Kennedy tried to play the "Senate man" by attending to these traditional matters and still act as an advocate of Democratic policy in opposition to Nixon. But in time he simply failed miserably in both roles. He neglected service to his Senate colleagues, and he became impatient with tedious administrative duties and favor-currying. During the pivotal year of 1969, his personal life began to absorb more of his time. He appeared to be preoccupied and to withdraw from the world (as well as from his Senate duties) in the aftermath, first of Robert Kennedy's assassination, and then of Chappaquiddick. As soon as he was linked with Mary Jo Kopechne's drowning that summer, long-suppressed questions about his character and socializing were made public, and Kennedy had to spend a great deal of his time explaining his behavior and defending his reputation.

His Senate career fared badly during the 1969 session. He was absent from the Senate forum more than present during that period, and at times his absence contributed to the defeat of vital liberal issues. In one instance, opponents of the anti-ballistic missile (ABM) system lost the fight against a Nixon-backed bill by one vote in August 1969. Kennedy was closely identified with the fight because he had sponsored a book (and written the introduction to it) that detailed the technical and political arguments against the ABM. Maneuvering within the Senate continued for months while Kennedy remained in Hyannis, dealing with the aftermath of Chappaquiddick. He returned to Washington too late to be of any help.

Kennedy was so negligent about his duties as whip that many senators questioned his capacity and right to maintain the post. He spent many hours in his home state campaigning for re-election to the Senate because he hoped to show by the returns that Chappaquiddick had not adversely affected his political career in Massachusetts (he won by a landslide). This took up so much of his time that staffers were left to fill the whip's duties. He and his staff made several blunders. Kennedy, for example, infuriated Majority Leader Mike Mansfield of Montana and other senators by bringing a consumer protection bill forward for consideration without notifying the interested senators. One of them, who happened to be a Kennedy supporter, lamented, "The simple truth is that Teddy just didn't do his homework." The number three man in the party, Senator Robert Byrd of West Virginia, was incensed at the condescending treatment he often received under Kennedy. By the end of 1970 Byrd said, "Sometimes I can't even make a routine motion. This has been going on for two years. I just have to sit there and take it!"

Kennedy was unable to pursue his goal as party spokesman. Immediately after Chappaquiddick, he was in no position to lead the attack against President Nixon on "moral" issues such as the Vietnam War. In fact, Kennedy was himself the target of attack by the White House during this period, having long been considered an "enemy" and chief political rival by President Nixon. Columnist Jack Anderson reported in 1974 that Nixon "began seeking political ammunition to use against Kennedy and Larry O'Brien. The orders were transmitted through staff chief H. R. Haldeman . . . Less than six hours after Kennedy ran off the bridge at Chappaquiddick on July 18, 1969, Jack Caulfield (a Haldeman appointee) had a man at the scene searching for evidence that could be used to embarrass Kennedy." Then later, "Caulfield kept Kennedy under surveillance during a three-day visit to Honolulu on August 17–19, 1971. A secret surveillance report which referred to the Senator as EMK was rushed to the White House . . . 'No evidence was developed to indicate that his conduct was improper,' " it said.

Senator Byrd began to take up the slack for Kennedy during this period and performed many of the services for his colleagues that the whip was supposed to handle. In contrast to Kennedy, he frequented the halls of Congress and took pleasure in the day-to-day operations of the Senate. It was only natural that he should challenge Kennedy formally for the majority whip post in 1971. Most of the senators, even those who voted for Kennedy out of loyalty, obviously agreed with a colleague who said, "Bob Byrd would do even the smallest chores for senators. Ted Kennedy didn't do a damned thing for anybody!" Kennedy was defeated by a narrow margin (31–24).

Kennedy's peculiar and remiss behavior as majority whip gave rise to a number of theories about his motivation and career goals. It is possible that he found himself faced with the need to decide between two career paths at this particular juncture: that of a powerful Senate insider, or that of a national policy leader. Kennedy, unlike the majority of politicians in American history, had the opportunities and capacity to move either way in 1969. The very peculiar and idealized relationship between the American people and the Kennedy family would support his drive for national leadership. On the other hand, his record in the Senate, his natural ability to deal with Senate norms and procedures and the respect with which he was held by senatorial colleagues drew him toward becoming a member of the Senate establishment. Kennedy had not decided which route to take or perhaps hoped that he could take both routes. His failure as whip made it obvious that these routes were mutually exclusive.

The untimely death of Robert Kennedy might have made the path of national leadership a more compelling choice. Kennedy's neglect of his duties as whip could have been a result of his growing ambivalence about the post as much as his temporary post-assassination withdrawal from public life. If this interpretation is accepted, Chappaquiddick was largely an irrelevant concern at the time. If Kennedy had functioned well as whip before and after the accident, many senators would have supported him and protected his position. The assassination of Robert Kennedy perhaps liberated the youngest Kennedy, allowing, or perhaps even forcing, him to take center stage in the national arena and to act as his own man, no longer encumbered by the demands of family.

One might also view Kennedy's defeat in the majority whip race as a fortuitous event that allowed him to resolve his ambivalence without having to make a conscious personal choice. Since he willfully neglected his duties as majority whip, the decision had already been made, but he left it to his Senate colleagues to actually force him in the direction toward which he had been moving for several months. His future was not to be that of an establishment leader of the Senate, but rather as a national leader. Thus it becomes less puzzling that Kennedy was so quickly adopted by Democrats as a leading national spokesperson.

After his defeat by Senator Byrd, Kennedy retired to the back benches of the Senate once again and began to assemble a large staff of experts for his various subcommittees. The staff work was an important part of Kennedy's plan to establish his expertise on "national" issues, advance his reputation as a leading Democratic spokesperson, and prepare himself for the presidency. He was strict with his staff and demanded that they prepare background work in detail and keep him well briefed. He also went to great lengths to assuage whatever bad feelings his colleagues might have for him as a negligent majority whip and to build on the relationships that were obviously essential for his political advancement.

Since 1972 Kennedy has become a political "godfather" of sorts in the Senate. When favors are needed or influence must be procured, many colleagues and lobbyists go to him, for he has been known to help senators with requests and favors for important constituents whenever he can.

Largely because he has the money and the staff to deal with them, he is able to handle many of these requests. Besides ingratiating himself with his colleagues in these ways, Kennedy also lends his name to re-election campaigns of fellow Democratic senators and makes innumerable speeches in their behalf. Over the years he has amassed a fortune in favors, which were readily convertible into votes.

In an analysis of the legislature called *Who Runs Congress?* Nader protégé Mark Green called Kennedy "the most influential Senator of the decade" because he is a master at working the Senate system. Style has much to do with influence, and Kennedy has cleverly learned how to be persuasive and personable with his colleagues. This is one of the qualities that sets him apart from President Carter, Green noted, since their methods of operation are poles apart. "When he's involved on an issue, Kennedy simply calls people over the phone to mobilize them if he needs support, whereas Carter doesn't like to use the telephone and hasn't been very good at that sort of thing."

Kennedy's relations with most of his fellow senators today are congenial. He gets along well with liberals and conservatives; he worked closely with James Eastland (before his retirement from the Senate) and does so now with Robert Byrd — an important maneuver, since Byrd, as the majority leader, is currently the number-one man in the Senate hierarchy. Byrd has been unremitting in his praise of Kennedy's Senate record ever since Kennedy declared his candidacy for the 1980 presidential election. The characteristics that Kennedy developed as the youngest child in an aggressive family have obviously served him well in the Senate. He has shown that being accommodating and congenial is most effective in working with his colleagues, even if the motivation for his behavior might be his own political advancement.

Relations with his Republican colleagues are diverse. Some GOP senators intentionally try to embarrass or contradict Kennedy in floor debate either to attract publicity or because of genuine ideological conviction. Some observers credit Kennedy with building a strong reputation in the Senate *despite* the fact that his name is Kennedy.

He is undeniably a more polished and capable institutional politician than brothers John or Bobby were and is careful to play both sides of the fence by alienating as few influential sectors as possible. Colleagues in the Senate, important journalists, and special interest group leaders are likely to receive occasional notes from him commending or castigating them on pertinent topics. Congressional sources cite his savvy and deft maneuvering within the system as one of Kennedy's greatest political assets. He tries hard to win his colleagues as much through the force of his personality as by principle and argument. Today inside the Senate he is considered a very able establishment figure, particularly because of his staff work.

A cursory look at his standing with "liberal" groups can be deceptive. The Americans for Democratic Action gave him 95 percent approval on his voting record for the 1976–1979 period, but he has been sharply criticized by the American Civil Liberties Union for provisions in his criminal-code revision that they consider to be an infringement on civil rights. In this area, Kennedy has staked out a new position that does not fit easily into either the traditional liberal or conservative camps. He has also been attacked by Ralph Nader's Congress Watch, a consumer group that monitors legislation in Congress, for compromising so heavily on his bill to reform the drug industry. Several Washington columnists and consumer groups were appalled at concessions to large corporations included in the anti-merger bill. Some attack him for being too accommodating in order to ensure passage of bills, while colleagues often claim that Kennedy seeks publicity by encroaching on the work of other committees and then neglecting to follow through.

Kennedy was the darling of "liberal" and progressive constituents before he became a presidential candidate. His work on the Judiciary Committee was initially more consistently favorable to consumers and the general public in the areas of civil rights and antitrust. He was responsible for several important provisions of the Freedom of Information Act and successfully led the fight to override President Ford's veto of that bill. After conducting oversight hearings on the Civil Aeronautics Board, Kennedy championed the deregulation of the airline industry, which resulted in lower air fares for consumers. He repeatedly opposed Senator Russell Long's attempts to create tax loopholes for corporations and the wealthy. Nader wrote of this, "Though he lost many of these votes, his challenges received considerable media attention and slowed down the Louisianan oil baron. Sneaking through privileged tax amendments for specific industries or companies is a little more difficult now because of Kennedy's disclosures and firm stands."

However, in 1979, with the presidential campaign in sight, Kennedy moved away from his liberal posture. The national health insurance bill, which he nurtured for years, now looks more like President Carter's own health bill and less like the bill promised to labor leaders and consumer groups. Nader and his colleagues were upset with Kennedy's compromise on the Drug Regulation Reform Act. Labeling it "the drug industry relief bill of 1979," Nader wrote:

> Having conducted some of the finest oversight hearings on the FDA in congressional history, Kennedy and his staff had the evidence to really tame a drug industry that was too slipshod in safety, too deceptive in its claims and too exorbitant in its prices. Instead, after Kennedy's acceptance of thirty-nine industry-desired amendments sponsored by Sen. Richard Schweiker, R-Pa., S. 1075 . . . weakens the power of the FDA to protect the public and broadens the ability of the drug manufacturers to keep test results secret and to stall.

The original drug industry bill of 1978 was substantially more favorable to consumers. However, in order to secure more Republican support for the bill, Kennedy agreed to concessions insisted on by Senator Schweiker, so that the bill now bears little resemblance to its original version. Nader opposed a provision that defines which information on safety must be released to the public. The bill requires only that summaries of test results on all drugs be made public, so that the drug companies can keep details of their research methods and results secret. The bill also allows the manufacturers to export drugs that are not approved for domestic use to foreign countries. Kennedy, who claims to be concerned about the poor around the world and includes provisions in his health bills to help them, would allow the drug companies to reap great profits from unsafe drugs in these poor countries. Ironically, the Nader consumer group considers the Carter administration's bill on the same subject more palatable than that of their usual champion (Kennedy).

Another example of Kennedy's willingness to compromise and his retreat from liberalism is his failure to continue the attack on "expense account living." He used to claim that U.S. taxpayers had to cover close to 75 percent of the costs of expensive business lunches, theater tickets, and first-class airline seats because of tax loopholes for big business. In an interview with an *Esquire* writer in March 1979, he said, ". . . I'm against cutting out school lunches for the needy to preserve three-martini lunches for businessmen." This was largely his way of using metaphor to explain his emphasis on tightening tax loopholes to raise government revenues instead of cutting back on social programs. But since declaring his candidacy and in response to public preoccupation with problems in the economy, particularly inflation and recession, Kennedy has completely changed his emphasis. Instead of closing tax loopholes, which would discourage businesses, he has decided instead that industry needs a boost and that the government must "provide additional incentives to encourage capital formation." He does not specify what kinds of incentives he would propose, but is intent upon being perceived as the "leader" who could bring new life to the business world. He is clearly anxious to allay business fears that he would be a "left-of-center" President.

Before the campaign, Kennedy did not take issue with any of President Carter's major economic policies. Since becoming a candidate, he tried to separate himself from the President by drawing attention to the administration's economic failures over the last four years, but the actual alternatives Kennedy offers indicate how minimal are his differences in economic philosophy. In fact, as *New York Times* correspondent Hedrick Smith pointed out, even the Republican candidates take positions similar to Kennedy and Carter on the top issue of the day, inflation: "The similarity of their views has developed into a surprising consensus. In the eyes of leading Republicans and Democrats alike, "supply-side economics" — the promotion of savings, investment, growth and productivity — offers the principal long-term answer for inflation." None of the candidates originally advocated wage and price controls to check the soaring inflation rate. Kennedy approved of Carter's voluntary wage and price guidelines and had consistently opposed mandatory controls. But Kennedy is quick to criticize Carter for placing more emphasis on restraint by labor to keep wage increases down than on restraint by business to raise prices more slowly. Although wages did increase by about 8.3 percent during one twelve-month period with guidelines in effect, for example, prices increased much more. Kennedy claims that Carter pressures labor leaders more than business executives to restrain increases, and that "to battle inflation the President has to be in the thick of the battle." Beyond rhetoric, however, he has few specific plans in mind. He intends to place more pressure on business to curtail price increases if he is President. At the same time, he seeks ways of increasing productivity in American industry, for instance by creating more "incentives" for business to expand and instituting a "much more aggressive foreign-trade policy."

Kennedy accuses Carter of holding back from the battle against inflation and says, "It's Fred Kahn's battle against inflation, wages and prices" instead of Carter's. Since Kennedy himself is known to rely just as heavily on his top advisors, he is obviously referring to the "methods" he believes a "leader" must pursue. He implies that he would be more ambitious and diligent in taking the battle against inflation to the public and attempting to rally an ailing economy, again by force of his personality as much as by principle or policies. Indeed, he asserted that he had been forced to run for the executive office for that very reason: "When difficulties rise so large that they threaten the essential confidence of our nation, the energies of our people must be marshaled toward a larger purpose — and that can only be done from the White House . . . Yet we hear no clear summons from the center of power. Aims are not set. The means of realizing them are neglected." In the absence of more specific proposals to solve the nation's problems, Kennedy spends most of his time speaking in platitudes about his ability to inspire confidence, show strong leadership, restore idealism, and eliminate confusion as to who controls administration policies. He proposes, in short, to bring about an enormous change in attitude.

Kennedy supported President Carter's proposals to hold the federal budget deficit at $30 billion but complained that budget cuts were made in the wrong places and would hurt the poor and the unemployed more than any other groups. In the past, both men have favored tax cuts to stimulate the economy, but have been waiting to see how deep the recession may go before advancing more specific proposals. Again, Hedrick Smith noted, ". . . supply-side economics has become so accepted that, like the Republicans, [the Democratic candidates] also favor rollbacks in Social Security taxes, and tax cuts and credits to curb inflation and stimulate business and productivity."

Kennedy has been more successful at distancing himself from Carter's energy programs. He incessantly criticizes the administration's decision to decontrol domestic oil and natural gas prices as a surrender to the oil industry: "First, it has intimidated the Administration into throwing in the towel without even entering the ring on the issue of oil price decontrol. And second, it has intimidated the Administration into submitting a token windfall tax that is no more than a transparent fig leaf over the vast new profits the industry will reap." While many of these charges are valid, Kennedy has sought to capitalize on them before large audiences despite the fact that there are contradictions in his positions. He has also said, "we need greater competition within the energy system in this country, competition between existing fuel sources and through additional sources that come onstream." The man who championed the deregulation of airlines and trucks does not believe that deregulation of oil and gas will likewise benefit consumers, since only a few large companies stand to gain from such a move. His fervor for competition and deregulation is obviously a case-by-case approach rather than a consistent policy, and Kennedy proposes stepped-up government control in areas, such as energy and health, that affect everyone equally.

Kennedy has been able to use the energy issue more effectively than any other issue in the campaign thus far. The public is angry about the record profits of the oil companies, and the Energy Department provided more evidence to back up Kennedy's charges late in 1979 when it accused the nine major oil companies of overcharging consumers at least $1.2 billion during the energy crisis of 1973–1974. Again, he asserts that Carter has not shown strong "leadership" in advancing solutions to the energy crisis or fighting for his programs. Carter's Chairman of the Council on Wage and Price Stability, Alfred Kahn, advised the President to "ask" oil company executives to refrain from increasing prices, whereas Kennedy castigates the oil companies before his audiences at every chance he gets. He refers to Carter's 1976 campaign pledge to oppose the deregulation of oil and natural gas prices, and calls his about-face "the single action that contributes more to inflation than anything else." Kennedy would work to reimpose those controls if elected. He also charges that Carter has surrendered to the oil companies on the profits they could make after prices are decontrolled and implies that the President is anxious to pass whatever bill he can get through the Congress. But Carter tried to deflect this line of criticism by lobbying heavily to impose a "stiff" windfall profits tax on the oil companies. As the campaign progresses, the issue may affect the standing of the candidates. The nation is disgruntled with the lack of action on energy and fears the recurrence of gas lines. In August 1979, hundreds of thousands of auto workers walked off their jobs for six minutes to protest Carter's energy policies. They sent a barrage of postcards to the White House protesting the "rip-off" of American citizens by the big oil companies and OPEC. They demanded that price controls be reinstated on domestic crude and heating oils, a strong windfall tax be imposed on oil company profits, and a taxpayer-owned oil exploration company be set up.

Also in 1979, Kennedy made public a $58-billion energy plan that stressed conservation and grants to homeowners and businesses. It mandates direct grants of up to $300 for renters and owners to insulate and improve the efficiency of their residences. Businesses would be granted a maximum of $50,000 for the same purpose, and this would reduce oil imports by 4 million barrels per day in 1990 as well as create 400,000 new jobs where people live and work. This plan was inspired by an earlier plan instituted in Canada, which he claims has been successful: "They'll insulate 70 percent of their homes over the period of the next ten years and conserve 30 percent of their energy used in home heating."

Kennedy favors the development of synthetic fuels that can be used to supplement scarce energy resources, but he lambastes Carter's plan for such a program as being excessive. Carter had asked Congress for $88 billion in 1979 to establish a government corporation responsible for producing 1.5 million barrels of synthetic fuel oil per day in 1995. Kennedy called this a "spree of wasteful spending" and said extensive tests should be conducted before billions of dollars were spent. Because Kennedy again agrees with Carter on the proposals but differs over mere specifics, such statements demonstrate his attempt to ridicule the President's proposals on energy and to undercut his support. Kennedy's purpose here is to ensure that his own energy program will receive prominence in the media and in Congress. He claims that the administration should first expand the strategic reserve that the nation has on hand for energy needs in case of crisis (which is currently eleven days' worth of energy consumption). But since the two candidates are simply bickering over minor points of similar energy proposals, it is likely that they will cancel each other out in public debate.

Kennedy has castigated Carter for poor leadership because he bungled negotiations for oil and gas with Mexico and other countries. He proposes that under a new administration, the country could form alliances with Latin American countries to explore and mine energy resources in this hemisphere.

After the accident at Three Mile Island, Kennedy called for a two-year moratorium on nuclear plant construction until the costs and benefits could be studied more carefully. He has called for a separate federal agency to investigate nuclear accidents. "It is wrong to have the agency [Nuclear Regulatory Commission] that sets the standards assess the success or failure of its own rules in an area where human life is at stake." This is a particularly useful issue for him in the campaign before the right audiences (that is, the young or environmental groups).

According to Kennedy, Carter has done literally nothing enlightened or progressive about energy. He promised in 1976 to oppose decontrol of oil and natural gas prices and then supported decontrol. He promised in 1976 to support "legal prohibitions against ownership of competing types of energy" and then failed to propose a single measure to carry this out. Above all, he promised in 1976 to develop a viable energy policy, and four years later nothing conclusive has been done. The subject figured largely in Kennedy's announcement that he would be a presidential candidate: "Everyone agrees that we need an energy policy. But not just any policy. We need a policy which has not yet been put in place, one imaginative enough to bring our citizens to conserve old sources of energy while we speed the pursuit of new forms of energy, including power from the sun."

Many different sectors have been voicing their disenchantment with the President. Some labor leaders criticized him for failing to deliver the promised comprehensive health insurance plan, for tilting toward upper-income groups in the 1978 tax bill, for his inability to push welfare reform through Congress, and particularly for his failure to advance a workable energy program. Consumer leaders felt deceived by Carter's 1976 campaign promises, and Nader charged that "Carter's lack of effective support for consumer legislation has been half incompetence and half lack of interest." And though business leaders blame the recession in part on his hollow policies, they are delighted that he turned out to be a southern conservative on economic issues instead of a free-spending liberal.

But whether these critics of the President will buy Kennedy's assertions that he is the stronger leader is another matter. Kennedy's record of leadership in the Senate pleases many progressives who are disenchanted with the President. Kennedy's earlier successes in the Congress — the civil rights initiatives, freedom-of-information clauses, airline deregulation battles, and foreign-policy statements — showed a consistency of "liberal" principles. But such has not been the case in the last year or two. His more moderate line on big business, the hard-line approach to criminal-code revision, and the blatant compromises on drug industry reform, antimerger laws, and national health insurance confuse many staunch supporters. They are obvious moves to the political center during an election year so that he may gain more wide-ranging voter support and deflect "leftist" labels from critics. Though Kennedy backers still believe that his heart lies with the "liberals" and that he would be more bold on progressive issues once the election is over, it is not certain that he would be able to force "liberal" programs on the Congress even if he were President. At the very least, Kennedy claims, on the basis of his Senate record, that he is qualified to lead because "I have learned the necessary ways of persuasion and conciliation. I have learned to deal with the continental diversity of interests that my colleagues have been elected to represent."

Close friends like John Culver of Iowa and former Senator John Tunney from California have professed loyalty to Kennedy for years. A large number of liberal senators have also worked closely with him on numerous issues and solicit his help in their home states. Conservatives like Senate Majority Leader Robert Byrd praise Kennedy's Senate record, and his working relationship with House liberals is equally good. He is a close friend of House Speaker Tip

O'Neill, and many other Democrats flock to his support when he seeks cosponsors in the House for his bills. Most of his colleagues agree that he knows the ways of Congress as well as any of them.

But he has made enemies on Capitol Hill as well, often because of his own or his staff's aggressiveness and their desire to gain pre-eminence on issues of national concern rather than working with others in the Congress to achieve solid results. Kennedy tries to maintain a hold on all major national issues by hiring specialists for each topic or planting his own people on the important committees in the Senate, whether these fall under his jurisdiction or not. Issues that might not seem to touch his own home state of Massachusetts are important to him because every subject can attract more votes and media attention. His staffers choose to believe that this wide-ranging interest is generated solely by his deep commitment to the poor and the downtrodden around the country. Most of them are highly aggressive and ambitious, like the senator himself, and show a fierce loyalty when questioned about him. They speak like family members in terms of "we" when discussing the work or the campaign.

Although they are acknowledged as hardworking and capable by most other senators and staffers on Capitol Hill, Kennedy's staff has also created divisions and discord there. They try to monopolize work on important issues that might belong in other committees so that "their boss" will get the credit for it. They are accused of working solely for the good of the senator rather than for the good of the country. Toward outsiders who are not part of the Kennedy world, they can be pompous or patronizing. In much the same way his father encouraged contests among his children, Kennedy encourages his staffers to compete to have their programs or positions brought before him. He is able, as were his brothers, to elicit great loyalty and labor from his workers for very little reward. Even before he announced his candidacy in the fall of 1979, most of them were giving all their time to him, including weekends and holidays, hoping to propel him and themselves into the White House. In the last year or so, the drive for the highest national office has created a new reputation for Kennedy — as a workaholic rather than a playboy.

The glaring absence of women in important advisory positions in his office has been the subject of much controversy and speculation. Several feminists have charged that Kennedy's commitment to women is superficial and that he is obviously uneasy about working closely with them. He is considered "solid" by women's groups on important issues, since he favored Medicaid financing for abortions, actively supports the Equal Rights Amendment, and advocated the appointment of more women as federal judges. But because he has only recently appointed women to the higher posts in his campaign or Senate staffs, after much criticism from women's groups, Kennedy is viewed with suspicion. Even though Carter has been "good" about appointing women to high office, he is considered no better than Kennedy because of his reluctance to champion avidly issues important to women. Iris Mitgang, chairperson of the National Women's Political Caucus, said of the three Democratic candidates: "None of them are terrific in this area. I always have concerns about candidates' real commitment to women when they have no women close to them in policy-making positions." The fact that the National Organization for Women (NOW) decided to support Kennedy for the presidency probably reflects the hope that he will be more progressive on women's issues once in office than Carter is.

Kennedy's ability over his seventeen years in the Senate

to attract such a high-powered staff is often cited as evidence that he would be a good administrator as President. Several historians have suggested that, unlike Richard Nixon and Jimmy Carter, Kennedy is an extrovert without an inferiority complex, who has no qualms about surrounding himself with intellectuals and activists of various political shades. He hired, for example, Harvard Law School Professor Steven Breyer to be his chief counsel on the Judiciary Committee and Breyer was the man responsible for an extensive study that led to the deregulation of the airlines. A former Stanford University professor, Dr. Lawrence Horowitz, was largely responsible for the groundwork of the national health insurance program. On the other hand, Kennedy is sometimes criticized for being overprogrammed by his staff. One administration official responded to this by saying, "All of the senators are overprogrammed. They all have a huge appetite to take on many issues, so that they essentially have to be. But it's a good attribute to be highly programmable, which Kennedy certainly is. That's a large part of the job of the presidency. One just has to hope that a President will surround himself with good minds and then that he will make the tough decisions."

Over the years, Kennedy has proven to be a good administrator and an experienced Senate man, adept at the ways of influence and manipulation and at assembling political talent. Columnists have frequently charged that one of the biggest problems of the Carter presidency has been that Carter is unable to delegate work to experts and other advisors, that he insists on keeping everything to himself and working out problems without utilizing the staff and resources available to the President of the United States. In contrast, Kennedy seems able and willing to rely on legwork, evaluations, analyses, and advice from his staff people.

His ability to delegate work and organize his staff give strong clues about the manner in which he might function as an administrator if he were elected President. However, his erratic legislative record, which exhibits as many failures as successes, and his tendency to compromise may give many voters, especially confirmed liberals, pause for thought.

4

National Health Insurance:
Kennedy Liberalism

THE UNITED STATES has the dubious distinction of being the only advanced nation, with the exception of South Africa, that does not assure its citizens of adequate health coverage under national guidelines. Proponents of national health insurance argue that if the United States can pay for education and defense, for crime control and the arts, then it should also insure the health needs of its people. In the wealthiest country in the world, health resources are not only grossly maldistributed, but tens of millions of poor are left with little or no access to medical services. Minorities in the inner cities and individuals in rural areas are among the least cared for.

In 1979 the Department of Health and Human Services reported that 23 percent of the population, or 51.2 million Americans, were medically underserved. Thirty-one million of these people had no access at all to general-care physicians, and millions of Americans cannot afford to see a doctor even when it is absolutely necessary. Since the average American family of four spent close to $3500 in medical bills in 1979, it is obvious that relatively few can afford to satisfy their health needs without some type of insurance plan. But at least 23 million Americans have no coverage under any private health insurance plan, Medicaid, or Medicare, and therefore can hardly afford to be ill under any circumstances. Most of these people have an annual total family income under $10,000.

Obviously it is the poor who suffer the most from the inequities built into the system of privately financed medicine. In 1979, members of the Subcommittee on Urban Health Care for New York State explicitly made this point: "It is the medically unserved themselves who continue to suffer the greatest effects of all these barriers to care. Despite the national life expectancy of seventy-three years, a review of death and communicable-disease statistics for medically underserved communities discloses rates of disability and mortality that are often many times higher than national average figures." People who reside in medically underserviced communities often suffer for their poverty, for they may be unable to pay for service and so are automatically denied treatment, because doctors and hospitals generally demand to see insurance or Medicare cards before patients are permitted to enter.

The costs of illness far exceed the average American's ability to pay. In 1965 medical bills of all kinds (hospitals, doctors fees, lab tests) amounted to $38.9 billion, or 5.9 percent of the Gross National Product, whereas in 1979 that total was in the vicinity of $206 billion, or 9.1 percent of GNP. The price of a hospital bed in Massachusetts General Hospital, which was $80 a day in 1969, more than doubled by 1979 to $199 a day. The health care industry is the nation's largest conglomerate, with annual revenues exceeding even that of the military-industrial complex by more than $50 billion. While many people are unable to pay for care, hospital construction and attendance at medical schools have expanded at such a high rate and so many new facilities have been created that at any one time about one-fourth of the hospital beds in this country are empty.

Partly this is because many of the beds are not in the locations in which they are needed. Rather than there being a dearth of doctors, the problem lies in their geographic distribution, according to the New York State Health Subcommittee members.

> First, while the number of graduates may be increasing, most of our new physicians are continuing the trend of practicing specialized medicine, not the kind of family-oriented general health care that the HEW data indicate is the real need . . . Second, the graduation of more medical students will not solve the maldistribution problem. Without stronger incentives and redefined priorities, physicians will not for the most part willingly practice in the inner city and rural areas.

Because the medical industry does not quite operate under classic free-market conditions of competition, costs and services are difficult to control. It is a seller's market, in which the buyers (patients) are told what they need and how much they must pay for it. Doctors have a monopoly on the services they perform, for patients cannot diagnose or treat their own illnesses, and without a system for peer review, the consumer has no basis on which to judge the physician's performance. Patients have little choice but to accept the services offered and the fees charged. The American Medical Association sets the standards for medical school admissions and licensing boards, which govern the most prestigious and powerful professions in America. The AMA, physicians, medical service unions, pharmaceutical companies, and private health insurance companies are tightly bound in professional associations to protect the interests of the sellers. The wider public is left without any form of control.

Over thirty years ago the more liberal wing of the Democratic party concluded from this state of affairs that the government should take more responsibility in aspects of the health system. Harry Truman introduced the first national health plan in the late forties, and many others have appeared since the original. Each of these proposals was based on the assumption that the delivery of medical services (by hospitals and doctors) should remain in the private sector and should not be "nationalized" in any sense of the word. However, the plans did generally differ about whether the sources of funding for the program should be public or private and how wide the extent of national coverage should be.

Edward Kennedy's plan closely resembles those drafted by other members of his party. Kennedy was assigned to the Senate Subcommittee on Health and Scientific Research in 1963 and later became chairman in 1971 by outmaneuvering three other senior members. His staff and medical experts then began to map a strategy for revamping the health care system in the country. Because of the importance and complexity of the issue, and because national health was to become a hallmark of Kennedy's career, the entire field was carefully researched, testimony was taken, and experts prepared elaborate studies. Kennedy conducted dozens of hearings around the country on "the health care crisis in America" and took his Health Subcommittee to nine American cities and several European countries in an effort to evaluate a variety of programs.

After the hearings in 1971, a book appeared under Kennedy's name titled *In Critical Condition: The Crisis in*

America's Health Care. Much of the book consisted of experts' testimony given before the subcommittee, where witnesses told of the financial ruin that resulted from catastrophic illnesses. The witnesses were largely middle-class Americans with above-average incomes. Kennedy summarized his goals after the hearings: "No American in our affluent age should be forced to mortgage everything he owns for health care . . . We will never eliminate illness and injury, but we can lighten their financial burden . . . the costs that would destroy any one of us are small when spread among all of us according to our ability to pay. I believe it is worth it. We can do this for one another, and we should."

Kennedy's grand scheme for national health insurance evolved from these hearings. The latest version of his plan was introduced in September 1979 and was titled the Health Care for All Americans Act of 1979 (S. 1720 and H.R. 5191). The bill would provide all citizens and permanent residents of the United States with most basic health needs, such as unlimited hospital care, physician and lab fees, and x-ray and medical equipment costs. Eligible people would be expected to enroll in one of four different plans: a commercial insurance company plan, a Blue Cross/Blue Shield plan, a health maintenance organization, or a self-insurance plan (such as Taft-Hartley funds). Individuals would choose the plan they prefer and then receive a health insurance card that entitled them to payment for benefits covered. The card would not indicate the patient's source of payment or income bracket so that these data could not be used as a basis for discrimination.

The delivery of health care (doctor and hospital services) would remain in the private sector. However, contrary to some of the earlier health plans, this proposal does not mandate public financing of health care but keeps funding under the control of the private sector as well. Neither hospitals nor doctors would be susceptible to government control. The insurance industry, heavily regulated by the government, would administer most of the program, so funding would not come directly from government sources. The four plans would have to offer individuals a comprehensive benefit package, but individuals would be free to choose their own physician. Both employers and employees would jointly pay for coverage; employees would pay a maximum of 35 percent of the cost of the policies, and employers would pay the remainder. Payments would be adjusted to employee income and the value of the benefits package, and the employers' share would be related to the size of their payroll. The government would step in only to subsidize small employers and to take care of individuals who are not employed full-time. Workers would be able to bargain, through union contracts, for stipulations that employers must pay the full price of the premiums.

Health maintenance organizations (in which groups of doctors practice and subscribers pay a set monthly fee for all medical services) and participating insurance companies would be required to cover any individual regardless of his health or economic status. These groups would be "encouraged to compete among themselves by putting together special packages with doctors and hospitals, in order to lower costs or improve benefits so as to attract buyers." The government would continue to fund and operate improved programs for the poor, the elderly, and the disabled. Medicare and Medicaid coverage would be expanded, so deductibles and copayments would be eliminated. Medicare patients would also be covered for prescription drugs and long-term nursing home care. State governments probably would save as much as $5 billion in Medicaid costs. Contributions from the general fund would relieve small employers of premium costs and also assure migrant workers, part-time employees, and other low-income working people of coverage. The actual financing for the plan therefore would come from payroll taxes paid by employers, a general fund drawn from federal and state taxes, and individual employees.

Costs would be tightly controlled in an attempt to put a lid on skyrocketing physician fees and hospital costs. State health boards would be set up, nominated by the governor of each state and confirmed by a National Health Board. The state boards would prepare an annual state budget, which would have to be approved by the National Health Board. The national health budget would allow expenditures to rise no higher than the average rate of inflation of the previous three years. Health service providers would have to negotiate rates of payment with employers, unions, consumers, and the government within the ceilings set by these budgets.

Proponents of Kennedy's national health plan emphasize that it will cost Americans less than they are now paying annually for scattered health services. They refer to it as a "rearrangement" of the way health care costs are currently paid. The Committee for National Health Insurance, a citizens' group, explained: "Under today's non-system, the individual or his family pays the doctor, the hospital, the insurance company or companies and frequently others. There are frequently deductibles, co-insurance and limitations in the insurance, and these have to be paid too. Under national health insurance, the costs are paid in full on the basis of advance negotiations."

If the act were made into law, a two-year lag would be

necessary to put cost control mechanisms in operation, and then benefits would be phased in. No additions would be made to the federal budget until 1983. In the first year in which the new system was operative, $28.6 billion would be added, and business and workers would spend for the plan about $11.4 billion more than they do now. For the first four years after benefits took effect, costs would be higher than those of existing programs for health services. Ultimately, however, costs should be lower under a national health care system because of the controls, the increased competition, and the greater efficiency of the system. Supporters project that health costs will be reduced by $31 billion in a single year by 1985. (They estimate that without a national plan medical costs will reach $361.6 billion by that year, whereas with national health insurance, the cost would be $330.6 billion.) The average American who now spends about $850 annually (or $3500 per family) for health would spend the same under a national health insurance plan, but in time the inflationary spirals in medical costs would be brought under more direct control. Americans with above-average incomes would spend slightly more for their health care and those who earn under the national average would spend slightly less.

Kennedy's earlier drafts of the national health insurance bill were quite different from his latest version. The original proposal was a labor-backed bill written jointly by physicians on Kennedy's staff and legislative experts in the AFL-CIO, the United Auto Workers, and the International Brotherhood of Teamsters. The proposal that Kennedy first advanced in 1971 was to be financed completely from the public sector, with half the funds drawn from general taxes and the other half from payroll taxes. But the Kennedy plan has always maintained the delivery of health services in the private sector. Under an intensely capitalist system, the American people and their politicians obviously would not accept "socialized medicine" in the sense that hospitals are government owned and operated (as in Great Britain). Kennedy revised the plan drastically over the years in order to placate hostile congressmen and a public that reacted badly to any plan that smacked of "nationalization," even if it was simply the funding of the program that would be shifted to the public sector. The insurance industry mounted a powerful and clever campaign against the early bill, and the Kennedy forces were hard put for some time to keep sentiment for national health insurance alive.

Kennedy lobbied heavily for public support of the plan, even speaking at several of the nation's prestigious medical schools because he wanted the support of medical academics for his plan. In 1975 he modified one of his bills that would require medical school graduates to practice in underserviced areas for a short time if their schools received federal grants. He agreed instead to sponsor President Ford's bill in the Senate, which required only 15 to 25 percent of the graduates of federally funded medical schools to serve in underserviced areas, a pragmatic move to make sure that at least parts of his proposals would be adopted.

Kennedy was forced to make further major compromises in 1977 when he attempted to work with President Carter in outlining a joint national health insurance plan. Carter set three conditions for his collaboration on a plan: that private insurance companies be allowed to run the bulk of the program, that the government's share of financing be kept to a minimum, and that the additional bureaucracy needed to operate a plan be minimal. Kennedy's Health

Subcommittee went ahead to model a new plan with these stipulations in mind. But because of the political competition between Kennedy and Carter and Kennedy's unwillingness to compromise as much as the President demanded, the two could not work together for long and each of them introduced separate national health plans in 1979.

Alterations in the Kennedy bill have disappointed the more liberal proponents of national health. When the latest version was sent to the Senate in 1979, AFL-CIO chief Lane Kirkland said that the previous versions had already incorporated enough compromises to "meet administration demands," including the reliance on the private sector for financing and delivery of medical services, the phasing-in of benefits, and the emphasis on cost control. Ralph Nader's Consumer Health Research Group switched their support from the Kennedy plan to a bill sponsored by Congressman Ronald Dellums that provides that the financing and the delivery of medical services should be completely in the public sector, or under government control. The consumer group is wary of any plan that allows private insurance companies as much control as Kennedy's does because members distrust the past performance and profit motives of these companies. Spokesmen argue that because a national health plan is years away, having no plan is better than having one that legitimates many of the more reactionary elements of the medical establishment.

Kennedy, however, has still not compromised to the degree that Carter has. As a candidate in 1976, Jimmy Carter spoke frequently of the inequities and inadequacies of the health care system. He promised to establish a comprehensive health care plan for all Americans if he were elected and wrote in his campaign autobiography, ". . . the quality of health care in this nation depends largely on economic status . . . Is a practical and comprehensive national health program beyond the capacity of our American Government? I think not."

Three years after he made these promises, the administration presented the long-awaited health care package. At first glance, the Carter formula looked very similar to Kennedy's. All Americans would be "assured" of basic medical services (hospitalization, physicians' fees, lab and x-ray tests). Workers would have to enroll in private plans for these benefits and would pay $2500 or more of medical costs themselves before the coverage began. The employee's share of premiums cost could not exceed 25 percent, and employers would pay the balance. The "small" number of part-time or self-employed workers, and other individuals not covered by private insurance plans could buy Health Care coverage. Health Care is the program that would be created from the merger of Medicare and Medicaid and would be designed primarily for the poor and the elderly. The groups eligible for this plan would expand to include people whose income is less than one-half that of those below the poverty line, which was $4100 for a family of four in 1979.

The program would force employers to buy insurance for agricultural and retail trade workers and others who are not well insured; if employers failed to do so, they would be subject to tax penalties. The plan would generate at least $10 billion annually in new business for private insurance companies.

Rather than submitting a complete plan before the end of his term as he had promised, Carter introduced a "first phase" program upon which he could build at a later date. If the Carter bill were to become law in 1980, benefits would not become available until after 1982.

The differences between the two proposals are significant. The President's plan would, in effect, establish two parallel health care systems whereby the poor would be forced to use public facilities and less well paid doctors, but Americans with the means would pay $2500 of their own medical expenses prior to receiving other coverage. Those employed full-time would carry private insurance instead of subscribing to Health Care and would visit private physicians who set their own fees, so that the chances that they would receive superior care would be high. The opportunities for discrimination against lower-income Americans are substantial in the Carter plan, because they alone would be forced to use Health Care facilities. All but the most destitute families would have to pay $2500 out of their own pockets before receiving any coverage, and this could amount to as much as 25 percent of a family's annual income.

The administration plan also offers a more restricted range of benefits. The Carter plan does not provide outpatient drug coverage for chronic diseases under Medicare, nor does it include as much coverage for mental health care as the Kennedy plan. Provisions for preventive services cover only the first year of a child's life, whereas the Kennedy plan provides for children to the age of eighteen. The programs also differ substantially in terms of how they would be financed. The Kennedy bill distributes medical care costs over a large population by drawing funds from payroll and general taxes. An individual's payment for coverage is related to his income, and individual contributions are limited to the actual health insurance value. But the administration plan basically aims toward expanding the Medicaid program with increased funding, participation, and benefits, and under the Carter plan, an individual's payment would not be related to his income, and his coverage would not begin until he had paid $2500 out of pocket.

But more-symbolic differences underlie the very nature of the plans. President Carter retreated from his original promise to provide a comprehensive national health insurance program and decided instead to propose an expansion of existing programs, which will not relieve the burden of large medical expenses for poor families or effectuate national budgeting for health care. Without an annual national budget plan for health care (which Kennedy's plan mandates), the Carter plan does not provide for government initiatives to limit rapidly rising medical costs. Carter is instead relying on his hospital cost containment bill to limit these expenses. This bill, which has been languishing in Congress for three years, would give hospitals a deadline, by which time they must show that they could voluntarily curtail their own costs. If hospitals failed to keep costs to an average annual increase of approximately 10 percent or below, with an adjustment for inflation, the President would be allowed to impose mandatory controls. Carter estimates that this could cut $40 billion from the nation's health bills over the next five years.

Supporters of national health are disappointed by the Carter plan for many reasons, one of which is that it does not motivate physicians to practice in areas where care is inadequate. An expert in national health who advised Kennedy compared the two plans.

> [Our] fee schedules will be adjusted annually to encourage physicians to practice in medically underserved areas. Similar incentives will be used to encourage physicians to practice in primary care specialties. The Administration's bill assumes that physicians will accept Health Care fees, although public payment presently constitutes only 28 percent of physician income.

Because Health Care fees will be fixed and private payment will not, there is a strong possibility that physicians will not treat Health Care enrollees. It is likely that access to private physicians by Medicare and Medicaid enrollees will be even more limited than is the situation today.

Kennedy has thus far refused to compromise on some basic principles of his national health plan to which he has retained a deep commitment. These include the provisions for universal coverage, comprehensive benefits, across-the-board controls such as national budgeting, and reforms to promote health maintenance organizations and preventive services. His commitment to an extensive program is obvious from his critique of the Carter plan: "By failing to set a national budget, by inadequately controlling hospital costs, by failing to control doctors' fees in the private sector, by creating two separate and unequal systems of care, the President's plan may well become the straw that breaks the back of the American health care system."

Both plans differ substantially from those instituted years ago in Great Britain, West Germany, and other European countries. The British system is highly centralized and seeks uniformity of practice throughout the country. Most physicians are directly employed by the government, and most hospitals and other medical centers are under national control. The Kennedy and Carter proposals guarantee decentralization by allowing states and local communities to operate health plans autonomously. American physicians would continue to practice privately, hospitals would remain in private hands, and private insurance companies would operate most of the programs, whereas in Britain these programs are publicly controlled. Under the British system, the nation's health costs amounted to 5.6 percent of the Gross National Product in 1977 (the last year for which data were available), as compared to 9.1 percent of GNP in the United States.

The British system, however, has numerous critics who frequently claim that the system has serious defects, despite the fact that the great majority of the British public approve of their health system. One of the most urgent problems is the loss of physicians, who have migrated to other countries in search for higher salaries. And patients who wish to undergo elective surgery that is not especially critical for their health must frequently wait three to six months to be scheduled for operations.

Kennedy has periodically consulted Canadian experts on national health and has incorporated aspects of the Canadian system, which went into effect in 1968, into his own plan. As he lobbies for national health insurance proposals, Kennedy frequently presents Canadian data to demonstrate that under the national health plan, the life expectancy rate of Canadians rose and medical costs declined. In 1965 both Canada and the United States spent 5.9 percent of GNP for health care, but in 1977 the Canadian national health program cost 7 percent of GNP, whereas private health care in America amounted to 8.9 percent of GNP. Polls taken in Canada in 1979 show that 84 percent of those interviewed approved of the health care system.

Kennedy realized that the Canadian experience could be used to educate Americans on the need for national health, and after a fact-finding trip to Canada, he publicized these results in committee hearings around the United States. The thrust of his message was that Canadian national health not only works, but is far superior to the American system in three areas: the percentage of the population covered by health insurance, the lower annual costs per patient, and the higher proportion of hospital beds, physicians, and nurses per 100,000 people. The Canadian system maintains the delivery of medical services (that is, hospitals and physicians) under the private sector, as Kennedy's plan does, but uses government revenues to finance the program directly instead of relying on private insurance companies.

Kennedy argues that national health has succeeded in other nations and that a national health insurance plan would prove to be markedly superior to private health care in America. It would, for example, greatly curtail "cheating" throughout the medical system. Health experts in this country estimate that more unnecessary operations are performed in the United States than in any other nation. The Public Citizens' Health Research Group filed suit in 1978 to force medical groups to publicize their information on doctors and hospitals participating in federally funded programs. The research group won, and the information that was made public revealed that large numbers of patients were admitted to hospitals for questionable operations at government expense. A General Accounting Office study showed that the Office of Personnel Management could limit health costs of Americans if requests for operations were more carefully scrutinized. Several federal employee insurance plans now require a second opinion for nonemergency surgery.

Doctors' incomes have risen so dramatically in the past twenty years that the annual median income is now $65,000, which is substantially higher than that of attorneys and most other licensed professionals. Increases in physicians' incomes would be less steep under the Kennedy plan because doctors would be required to bargain with state and local health boards and insurance companies before setting their fees. Through various incentives, physi-

cians would also be discouraged from admitting more patients for prolonged hospital stays, from prescribing
excessive medical tests or drugs, and from performing
questionable operations. Insurance companies would be
discouraged from practices such as paying for lab tests
only if they are conducted on the seriously ill, that is, on
hospitalized patients. The national health plan, in short,
would impose more incentives and controls for curtailing
costs in an industry that otherwise operates freely with few
limitations.

Opposition to most national health insurance plans, particularly Kennedy's, is formidable for this very reason.
Scores of private-interest groups refuse to allow the government to curb their profits in any way. The American
Medical Association, the most powerful opponent of national health, will fight any national policy that allows
Congress and the government to interfere with the practice
of medicine. The American Hospital Association, hospital
workers, and nurses' unions, as well as other organized
groups, also oppose the plans for the same reasons. The
Health Insurance Association of America, the umbrella organization of all private insurance companies, is unhappy
with a bill like Kennedy's (although his most recent version
is more acceptable to them) because insurers are anxious
about the long-term implications of federal regulation of
their businesses, which are now primarily regulated by the
states. The major pharmaceutical companies have less to
be concerned with, since the Kennedy bill does not mandate drug coverage, but the pharmaceuticals would probably support the AMA and other medical groups because of
their commonality of interest. The manpower and money
that can be marshaled to prevent or delay health insurance
legislation is obviously great. The AMA and its supporters

run one of the most powerful and effective lobbies in Washington, which is the major reason why the United States does not yet have a national health program, more than thirty years after the idea was first conceived.

Kennedy and Carter have made extensive revisions and compromises on their original proposals, largely because of such opposition. At the same time, Kennedy's aggressive lobbying and pressure forced Carter to propose a health plan that is substantially more "generous" than he otherwise intended. Carter has defended the modesty of his program by saying that "the idea of all or nothing has been pursued now for almost three decades. It's time to rise above the differences that have created that stalemate and act now, this year."

The President has won the support of several key congressmen in the fight to advance his bill in the Congress. Congressman James Corman of California, who formerly worked with Kennedy for an all-public health insurance program, joined Carter after the President agreed to include a program for pregnant women and infants in the administration plan. Carter also won the support of the powerful Senator Russell Long. Long's allegiance is critical to Carter because, as chairman of the Senate Finance Committee, he controls the health budget and may well have the final say in determining health policy in the upper house. Senator Long had been interested in health proposals for years and has introduced his own bills, which provide for only very limited coverage in the event of catastrophic illness or accident.

In 1979 Long made it known that he would be willing to combine his bill with Carter's and support the President against Kennedy, particularly since Long and Kennedy have been bitter adversaries for years. Congress Probe, an investigative news service in Washington, discussed the politics of the situation: "Carter and Long hope to undercut the Kennedy plan, have Congress pass their joint proposal and take credit for national health insurance . . . Kennedy has reciprocated by drafting an energy plan of his own in an attempt to undercut Carter's legislative energy solutions."

Kennedy, however, can still claim a more impressive array of support for his bill. When he first announced the plan in the summer of 1979, he was accompanied by a number of leaders of labor, black, farm, and religious groups, and senior citizens groups. He recruited as cosponsors a diverse group of senators, both Republicans and Democrats, among them liberals and several conservatives. And when his bill was introduced in the House by Congressman Henry Waxman of California, sixty other representatives signed as cosponsors, as opposed to three or four cosponsors for the Carter plan.

The possibility that any national health plan will pass the Congress in the next few years is poor. The AMA–pharmaceutical–insurance companies lobby is strong enough to affect the votes of numerous senators, and the simultaneous incidence of increasing antiregulatory and anti-inflationary sentiment in Congress today precludes sympathy for programs that require more government spending and control. Congress is generally reluctant to advance controversial legislation in an election year, and particularly in 1980, when a vote in favor of a Kennedy bill is a vote against the President.

Sympathy around the country for a major national health plan is also insubstantial in the wake of more pressing economic and energy problems. A few years ago many health experts were predicting that national health would soon be a reality, but very few would risk such a forecast today. Both Carter and Kennedy are finding it difficult to make health a major campaign issue in 1980. Neither can win many votes by claiming a legislative triumph since none is likely to occur before the election. But Kennedy, more than Carter, can refer to his years of work on health issues, emphasize his deeper commitment to disadvantaged Americans, and demonstrate his substantial mastery of the complicated health care issue before his audiences.

Several groups that remain committed to comprehensive public health programs have criticized Kennedy for moving too far away from programs most suited to consumer interests, particularly since he declared his candidacy for the presidency. They assert that Kennedy seriously compromised his health plan in 1979 because Carter attacked his inability to secure passage of health legislation for years as evidence of Kennedy's lack of "leadership" in the Senate. Ralph Nader wrote: "His various versions of health insurance have been moving closer to the deplorable Carter position as well as closer to what the health insurance industry and medical lobby find less objectionable." But many labor and minority leaders still recognize Kennedy as the champion of national health and the man most likely to lead the fight for national health if a legislative battle ever does occur.

Kennedy explained his concern about the health needs of all Americans in terms of his own personal experience. In the introduction to *In Critical Condition*, he wrote:

> I have personally tasted the tragedy of illness and injuries. In 1964 I survived a disastrous small-plane crash in which my back was broken and in which two other men were killed. I — and my family — suffered through a six-month hospitalization, during which I was immobilized on a striker frame, wondering

how disabled I would be and whether my career would end as a
result of the injury. My brother Jack returned from World War
II with a back injury that threatened to disable him and that
plagued him during his Presidency and all his life . . . We also
watched my father struggle through the last seven years of his
life with the crippling effects of a stroke. Our family knows only
too well the tragedy of illness and injury, and the deep personal
value of good health.

Added to these were the expenses for his wife's treatment
for alcoholism and their son's treatments for cancer.

Biographer James MacGregor Burns, an admirer of the
Kennedys, wrote that there were other, more complicated
reasons as well for Kennedy's long involvement on the
health issue: "Health . . . is a safe issue. If the Senator became a national leader, one Kennedy staff person said that
it was very possible that he would have 'no anti-poverty
program' as such, no program easily identified as black or
Chicano. The intent is to define issues in terms of universal
'human rights' that touch all the oppressed regardless of
race." In this sense, Kennedy hopes to win the support of
the poor and of minorities because he has championed a
significant form of "human rights" with a nonpartisan
issue. But the cause has made him susceptible to the
epithet of "big-spending liberal" and even of "socialist"
because of the implications of "equal health care for all"
and coverage for rich and poor alike.

In any case, Kennedy has so dominated the work on national health that he is almost unanimously recognized as
the "Mr. Health Care" of Congress. His Senate politics and
methods of operation became subjects of national promi-
nence largely because of his work in this area. The heavy
compromising, the public lobbying for support, the gathering together of numerous medical "experts" on his staff,

and the way he runs committee hearings are elements in a pattern that denotes Kennedy as "The Senate Man." His entourage of bright young people enabled Kennedy to outshine the President and other senators on health more effectively than on any other issue. Health care has been his most ambitious and highly publicized initiative, the initiative that solidified his image as the spokesperson of the disadvantaged. He has thoroughly researched this enormous subject and has remained with the issue for years despite its grim prospects in Congress. But he has earned this reputation at the expense of compromising his original position to such a degree that the United States may not have a truly comprehensive public health plan for many years.

5

Judicial Reform:
A New Conservatism

THE SENATE COMMITTEE on the Judiciary is among the most powerful in the upper house. It has jurisdiction over the appointment of federal judges, the regulation of business and antitrust laws, and the crucial legislation that delimits civil and constitutional rights. Membership in the committee has been a prime objective of ambitious senators because of the breadth of its jurisdiction, the extent to which it can affect the business and social life of the nation, and its potential effect on the Bill of Rights. Conservatives have often sought membership because it gave them an opportunity to block the appointment of liberal judges and civil rights legislation. In fact the committee was dominated for years by southern conservatives, with Senator James Eastland as the stalwart chairman who could always count on the support of fellow conservative southerners Strom Thurmond of South Carolina, James Allen of Alabama, and John McClellan of Arkansas.

That an ambitious freshman in Kennedy's position could make headway with progressive legislation and build his reputation in that domain is a substantial feat. He was able to achieve substantial power by befriending important members who might have silenced him, by working closely with them or lobbying cleverly when the need arose. He still gets along admirably with colleagues of various political shades, frequently appeasing troublesome members by cajoling and congeniality. At one meeting of the committee in January 1979, soon after Kennedy assumed the chair, Republican Strom Thurmond insisted stubbornly that one of his minor rule changes should be incorporated in the committee business. He repeated his proposal until Kennedy grinned at him, playfully shook him by the shoulder, and gave in, saying, "Strom, see how persuasive you are!"

Kennedy's accession to the chairmanship of the Judiciary Committee was abetted by the death or retirement of several key members and an increase in the number of liberal senators on the committee. He became the first chairman with a solid record in the civil rights area, and indeed the first liberal to hold the chair in decades. This is not to say, however, that Kennedy has been a steadfast champion of liberal causes or that his commitment to progressive reform has been continuous. Kennedy actively sought to dominate the committee as a high-profile activist by initiating liberal legislation in many controversial areas of public policy, despite his desire to please a national constituency with a large conservative component. He attempted to eliminate several subcommittees and create others in order to bring the business of the subcommittees more firmly under his control. He also tried to use his influence to recruit more liberal senators to the committee and substantially change its political complexion. His political sophistication was such that he cooperated closely with Republican colleagues when it came time to adopt the budget and the rules.

Within a few months of becoming the chairman, Kennedy introduced bills designed to restructure the Law Enforcement Assistance Act (LEAA) and a major bill to restrict potential mergers of big business conglomerates. In accordance with his interest in consumer rights, Kennedy scheduled hearings on the controversial "Illinois Brick" bill, which could revolutionize the relationship of consumers to producers by making it possible for secondary, as well as primary, consumers to sue producers. The process by which federal judges were selected also became a subject of heated controversy because of the attempt to lessen the input that individual senators on the committee formerly had. The committee was also considering amendments to Kennedy's criminal-code reform bill at that time.

Kennedy's activities on the Judiciary Committee were less disciplined by the tenets of liberalism than might appear. He steered a rather clever course, satisfying his more progressive supporters with his struggle for the Freedom of Information Act and measures designed to protect civil rights. But he later alienated large segments of this constituency when he seemed to be proposing the curtailment of certain rights under the criminal-code reform bill. At the same time that Kennedy proposed substantial restrictions on corporate mergers, he compromised his bills to appease business executives, and reiterated his preference for the sine qua non of conservative causes — free enterprise — when he launched a major campaign against government regulation of the trucking industry similar to the one he had waged to reduce government regulation of airlines.

Kennedy, like most flamboyant senators, is both a liberal and a conservative when it comes to steering his own course on a variety of issues. Part of the time this results from his conviction and principles, but he is never unaware of the political advantages that might be gained by adopting "correct" postures. Kennedy frightens businessmen with his proposals to restrict corporate mergers, but then, to appease them, he heavily compromises these proposals and at the same time rewards the business community by reducing regulation of certain industries. His liberal ideology has never been so firm that his political career would suffer during the pragmatic tests of conservative times. His advocacy of free enterprise in part runs counter to his New Deal philosophy, whereas his vigorous defense of government responsibility for the welfare of the poor conforms to that philosophy. But he has never paused to consider whether free enterprise might produce the need for welfare in the first place, having little time or inclination to examine searching political philosophies or to question the basic structure of the "system." His commitment to change rests simply on surface alterations, as is the case with all American politicians.

Kennedy's career on the Judiciary Committee illustrates how his conservatism and liberalism are in part politically motivated and in part the product of his liberal inheritance. When he became chairman of Judiciary, the business community expressed substantial concern that the committee would become a "Kennedy fiefdom" dedicated to the vigorous enforcement of antitrust legislation and civil rights. When Senator Eastland retired and fellow conservatives McClellan and Allen died, more liberal and younger Democrats replaced them, so that Kennedy had a comfortable working majority. He utilized this majority to advance the view that the central organizing principle of the American economy should be "free-market competition" protected by enforcement of the antitrust laws. Nobody disagrees with him in principle, of course, since free enterprise is the backbone and quintessential characteristic of American political culture. But Kennedy frequently propounds the doctrine as if he had come upon a unique first principle. His positions are platitudinous but extremely useful for a presidential candidate because they represent a remarkable compromise, entailing both free enterprise for businessmen and citizens who love patriotic themes, and a dash of trustbusting for progressives.

Kennedy's ability to promote legislation consonant with his political pragmatism was enhanced by a careful selection of the staff of the Judiciary Committee which, under his direction, became largely an adjunct of the chairman. Over 200 members of his committee staff prepare detailed studies, seek out numerous projects, and prepare hearings for his generally large audiences. Hearings directed by Kennedy are usually informative, though many are carefully staged for dramatic effect and favorable headlines. The staff briefs Kennedy with much care and supplies him with the copious data or questions he might ask or be asked, as well as the arguments that might be used against his case and counterarguments for his use. The briefings are extremely thorough, since the senator insists on performing well and avoiding the appearance of poor preparation. Kennedy is not an impressive ad lib speaker and sometimes improvises poorly by fumbling and hesitating. He is more fortunate than most politicians because he has the money to hire additional staff and he has the good judgment to recognize competence in others, a virtue not to be underestimated. It does become difficult, however, for the electorate to discern the identity and essence of a candidate fused with his entourage.

For some time after he joined the Judiciary Committee in the early sixties, Kennedy followed the protocol of the Senate and undertook no major projects, restricting himself to the business of the committee and only gradually defining himself as a liberal spokesperson. During the sixties, he concentrated on problems of civil rights and Vietnamese refugees. As chairman of the Subcommittee on Refugees, Kennedy publicized the plight of thousands who were fleeing from Vietnam, even though he did not avidly oppose the war for some time. In the area of civil rights here at home, he pushed diligently for more liberal voting laws and substantial revisions in the draft laws. He proposed legislation that would lessen discrimination against blacks and low-income groups in the Selective Service System, and then worked for years on a compromise with his committee colleagues and the Nixon administration until the bill became law in 1971. Kennedy demonstrated a forthrightness on this and other civil rights legislation not evident in his waffling position on the Vietnam War. He agreed, for example, to support the administration's draft bill only after he had received assurance that Senator Stennis would pursue more comprehensive reform of the Armed Services Committee.

In 1970 Kennedy and Senator Birch Bayh of Indiana maneuvered through the Congress the constitutional amendment that lowered the voting age to eighteen. Kennedy probably favored this bill both out of personal conviction and because he suspected that a younger electorate was more likely to become a Kennedy electorate. Electoral reform had been an earlier concern of Kennedy's when he led the efforts to ban the imposition of literacy tests and poll taxes, and to enforce the Supreme Court's one-man, one-vote decision.

In the early seventies Kennedy held hearings around the country on the proposed Freedom of Information Act. The bill guaranteed citizens unprecedented access to information collected by the government and designated as classified. As a result of the bill, the government became less ardent in its pursuit of information that was potentially harmful to citizens, while the public gained access to information that could prove to be a substantial protection against the state. For centuries governments have operated in secret because secrecy enormously enhances the freedom to maneuver and the ability to proceed without public scrutiny or condemnation. Therefore, that information can be a potent weapon, and Kennedy's support of the Freedom of Information Act was a major battle for the public's right to know, a landmark in legislative history, and may well turn out to be the most lasting achievement of Kennedy and his colleagues. His commitment to public rights also led him to become one of the key forces responsible for the successful effort to limit wiretapping by the government (allegedly for national security purposes) in 1977.

Though Kennedy had long been an advocate of vigorous enforcement of antitrust legislation, he was simultaneously committed to minimal government interference in the economy. His commitment to free enterprise became evident in the mid-seventies when he successfully led the effort to deregulate the airlines. When controls were removed, air travel became less expensive, and at the same time, the profits of the airlines increased. Kennedy was apparently so impressed by this benediction bestowed by free enterprise that he became more enthusiastic about deregulation, and soon turned his attention to the study of the trucking industry.

Perhaps the best way to understand Kennedy's moves is to interpret them as a modest populist crusade that has substantial political advantages. By supporting consumer rights on the one hand and government regulations on the other, and by breaking his own ground in a case-by-case approach, Kennedy is pursuing an effective strategy that divides the business community, earns him the support of progressive consumer advocates, and at the same time defies strict ideological labeling of "right" or "left." But though there was also much talk during John Kennedy's administration of limiting corporate power and economic freedom to bring about a more equitable distribution of the national wealth, the opposite situation resulted and corporate consolidation and control increased. The youngest Kennedy, like his brother, shows no deep commitment to altering this situation in any meaningful way.

Edward Kennedy's enthusiasm for deregulation grew from an idea that one of his staff members conceived in 1974. Stephen Breyer, counsel to the Judiciary Committee, wrote an extensive study of regulatory agencies, which impressed Kennedy. Commenting on Breyer's work, Kennedy summarized his new social philosophy of deregulation: "I am convinced that the key lies in agency-by-agency examinations of specific regulatory programs. Government bodies . . . should be guided by 'regulation as a last resort philosophy' . . . where health and safety are not paramount, and the industry consists of several firms in a reasonably competitive market, the most likely answer is not to regulate. Instead we should rely on the discipline of the market, backed by anti-trust policies."

Kennedy was so enthusiastic about this principle that in the summer of 1979 he introduced legislation that would require a critical study of each regulatory agency, an analysis of whether its activities were justified by market circumstances, and an evaluation of federal regulations in many areas. The business community, consumer activists, and labor sectors began to view Kennedy's activities favorably, proving that deregulation bridges both sides of the political spectrum — for conservatives it enhances free enterprise and for liberals it occasionally results in gains for consumers. One source of Kennedy's success as a politician lies in the selection of issues that appeal to widely different constituencies, and deregulation is just such an issue.

Following his initial success with deregulation of the airlines, Kennedy turned to the trucking industry. After lengthy hearings, he concluded that the industry need not be regulated as vigorously as it was, or in the same way that trains in the United States are. He insists that increased competition in trucking would result in lower prices and greater efficiency. The drive to deregulate the trucking industry was vigorously supported by representatives of the entire political spectrum: Ralph Nader, Alfred Kahn, and representatives of the National Federation of Independent Businesses.

But Kennedy, for the first time, was severely criticized by his colleagues and "disciplined" for the manner in which he was proceeding. Several senators charged that Kennedy and his staff had encroached upon territory of other committees. Some argued that Kennedy was being pulled in many directions by his aggressive staff and that he sought to gain the credit for many public issues that were the private preserve of others, simply to enhance his national reputation and presidential ambitions. His aides were described as "pushy" and "aggressive," and Kennedy was accused of attempting to create a "supercommittee." Several colleagues publicly complained that the Kennedy staff was overmanned and that their budget requests, $5 million annually, were excessive. Some even accused Kennedy aides of providing both questions and answers to witnesses who appeared before committee hearings and of eliminating witnesses who were recalcitrant or in opposition to their purpose. Several senators sought jurisdiction of the bill that affected the trucking industry, demanding that the bill be removed from Kennedy's committee and transferred to the Commerce Committee where the bill "rightly belonged." As Senator Ernest Hollings of South Carolina asserted: "The distinguished chairman of the Judiciary Committee, the Senator from Massachusetts, has been charging up to the parliamentarian for the last eight weeks with his very astute and tricky staff to say: 'How can we doctor this one and get it referred?' What we have is a total breakdown of the discipline, rules and proceedings of the U.S. Senate to grab hold of one thing." Kennedy eventually was forced to give way on the trucking bill and the bill was sent to the Commerce Committee.

In 1979, one year before the presidential election, Kennedy had staked his reputation on four crucial issues, all within the purview of the Judiciary Committee. He proposed a major change in the law that dealt with the right of consumers to file law suits for price fixing. Under existing law, only primary purchasers — wholesalers who purchase directly from a manufacturer — are currently permitted to sue. Kennedy's bill would permit consumers to sue even if they were the second, third, or fourth parties in the distribution chain. This bill has been nicknamed the "Illinois Brick" bill after a company that was originally sued for price-fixing, a case that eventually went before the Supreme Court. In that particular case, the Supreme Court ruled that under antitrust law only a primary purchaser could file suit against a manufacturer. The bill could represent a potent challenge to the monopolistic practices of big business and a boon to consumers. Because of the political implications of the bill and the good will of an army of consumers, the issue received top priority from Kennedy and his staff. In his report on the bill Kennedy wrote: "In the eighty-seven years prior to the 'Illinois Brick' decision, Congress and the courts had consistently recognized that consumers were the intended beneficiaries of anti-trust laws and that a private right of action for damages was provided with the express purpose of compensating consumers and others who paid the real cost of illegal conduct ". . . The central purpose of the anti-trust laws is to provide consumers better products at lower prices by maintaining competitive markets . . ." This bill is another manifestation of Kennedy's commitment to free enterprise. Business opposition to the bill is fierce because it could result in numerous consumer challenges to pricing practices, and business lobbyists fear that it would subject businessmen to endless "irresponsible" lawsuits. These lobbyists, as usual, were vastly better organized and more heavily funded than the consumer groups, which were slow to mount a defense. After intense lobbying, Kennedy let it be known that he would be open to major compromises. He was willing to alter the bill so that it would apply only to private businesses and state, local, and federal governments (publicly owned companies would be excluded), and he was even willing to eliminate the clause that made the bill retroactive for cases already pending in the courts. The compromises might be forthcoming in order to increase the chances that the bill will pass and to placate conservative business interests.

The senator had been involved in trustbusting ventures for years. In 1978 and 1979 he accelerated his attack on corporate mergers, but again it was a venture that illustrates his penchant for compromise. He initially proposed a bill to outlaw corporate mergers among firms with sales in excess of $350 million or assets of $200 million unless these firms could prove that an impending merger would increase competition and efficiency. The bill would also prevent mergers where either party controlled 15 percent of a given market. But it evoked violent protests from big businesses around the country, and when Kennedy met with corporate executives, he was persuaded to reintroduce a greatly weakened version of the bill. Columnist Jack Anderson reported that when the business executives voiced their objections to the bill, Kennedy aides "immediately began to rewrite the bill to meet some of the tycoons' demands." Anderson wrote: "It is unusual for the original draft of the bill to be watered down before it is even presented to the appropriate committees for hearings. The compromise and logrolling that are the standard features of the committee process invariably weaken a bill as originally written. Kennedy in effect was giving away bargaining chips before the game had even started." The haste with which he surrendered suggests, contrary to the Kennedy legend, an inability to confront adversaries and animosity. The youngest Kennedy, who was often afraid to disappoint or challenge older brothers and sisters, displayed an unsettling inability to confront pressure and seniority. The hasty and large-scale compromises that Kennedy made lead one to question his commitment to the bill and the principles underlying it. But he could defend his actions by arguing that he is less interested in curbing corporate power than he is in restricting profits and creating more favorable market conditions for consumers.

As was expected, the compromised version of the bill greatly disappointed consumer groups. In its amended form, the bill prevents only mergers among the 100 largest

U.S. companies that hold assets of at least $1.5 billion, and it also outlaws the merger of any two of the largest 500 companies unless they can demonstrate that the industry would be made more efficient by doing so. Kennedy defended his positions on the merger issue in an interview with *Esquire* magazine: "I'm not anti-business, I am pro-competition . . . I am against the concentration that's going on, the mergers and takeovers among the 500 biggest corporations in the country, and the tax laws and anti-trust laws that encourage those mergers. The end result of what is going on will be nationalization of major industries or the most strident kinds of government regulation. I don't want that to happen. So I think I'm saving business from themselves."

Kennedy had introduced close to fifty bills in 1979 alone. One of the most significant prohibits sixteen of the nation's major oil companies from purchasing any firms with assets in excess of $100 million for the next ten years. Kennedy has crusaded against the Seven Sisters — Mobil, Royal Dutch, Texaco, Socal Gulf, Exxon, and British Petroleum — more vociferously than any other candidate. His attacks on big oil, a popular topic with most Americans who blame the oil companies and OPEC for the nation's energy problems, are backed by his customary barrage of statistics. He reminds audiences of the high profits that the large oil companies reaped during the energy crises of the seventies. He describes their ability to manipulate world markets so as to maximize profits and influence nation states: "Oil companies own, in whole or in part, three of the top four coal producers. And fourteen of the top twenty holders of coal reserves are oil companies. The major companies continue to expand rapidly into other industries. Since 1973, oil companies have acquired firms with over $4 billion in assets in the mining and manufacturing sectors of the economy alone." He often summarizes by saying, "They alone among the institutions of the consuming nations have profited from the OPEC price increases."

Kennedy argues that the purpose of his bill is not to punish the oil companies but to encourage them to develop the oil, gas, and coal reserves they already hold and to seek new resources. His critique of the oil industry is illustrated in the following remarks.

> The timid response of the anti-trust authorities to coal and uranium acquisition has tempted the oil companies into ever broader acquisitions. Now they seek to escape notice in acquiring even their competitors in the oil industry itself. Two of the largest and most successful independent oil companies have been the targets of major companies. Gulf has successfully taken over Kewanee. And several major companies, Mobil in the lead, made an attempt to take over General Crude, a large multinational oil company in its own right . . . These are conglomerate mergers, they serve no purpose other than to bring completely unrelated activity (i.e. the acquisitions of packaging, food processing and publishing industries) together under one management. These mergers add nothing to the economy. They add nothing to the production of energy. They create no new assets. They create no new jobs. What they do create is bureaucracy.

He reminds his audiences that oil companies wield enormous power, not only in Washington but around the world, and often quotes Senator Hart of Colorado, who said: "When a major corporation in the state wants to discuss something with its political representatives you can be sure it will be heard. When the same corporation operates in thirty states it will be heard thirty times." Kennedy charges that the Department of Energy maintains a cozy relationship with the very industry it is supposed to regulate. He stresses the prospect that the petroleum industry is likely to make an extra $226.6 billion in profits when domestic oil and gas prices are decontrolled. This would occur, he emphasizes, at the time when oil profits are already astronomical and the consumer is heavily burdened with the costs of energy. For these reasons he criticizes President Carter relentlessly for lifting controls and argues that they should be reimposed. He also requested that the President support a stiff windfall profits tax on the large oil companies. The Carter administration, in turn, offers Kennedy only the mildest support for his antimerger bill.

Kennedy's attack on the oil companies has drawn plaudits from liberals and consumer groups around the country. But the very groups that support Kennedy in his efforts to control corporate mergers are shocked by his cosponsorship of a bill to revise the U.S. criminal code. The Kennedy bill is the legislative offspring of the infamous criminal-code reform bill sponsored by the Nixon administration, S. 1. Kennedy has repeatedly clarified his intention to take a firm position on the subject of crime control.

Questions about criminal-code revisions were first broached by President Johnson in 1964 when the White House requested a feasibility study. For over 200 years, the Federal Criminal Code has grown haphazardly whenever specific problems gave rise to specific laws, most of which were passed with little or no reference to preceding laws or general principles. Slight revisions were made in the code in 1877, 1909, and 1948, but no overall attempt to recodify the law was undertaken until Congress established a national commission on the subject, directed by former Governor Edmund Brown of California in 1966. The commission reported to President Nixon in 1971, and a bill regarded by many as regressive was submitted to the Congress in 1973. Numerous groups, including the American Civil Liberties Union, attacked the bill as the most significant modern infringement on First Amendment freedoms, and the bill quickly died in the Congress.

Kennedy surprised many liberal supporters in 1977 when he joined a block of Senate conservatives to sponsor a revision of the Nixon bill. Although some of the more objectionable provisions of the Nixon bill were deleted, civil liberties groups united in their condemnation of the Kennedy bill. The Senate passed the bill by an overwhelming majority the following year, but it was rejected by the House. The House Subcommittee on Criminal Justice did not deny that the code needed reform, but it did raise objections about the extensive revision requested by the Senate. Kennedy was determined to pass his bill, and the next year he coordinated his efforts with the House subcommittee. A revised version of the bill was reintroduced in 1979 with the support of conservative Republicans Strom Thurmond and Orrin Hatch of Utah. The bill itself, as well as the coalition of the leading liberal Democrat with conservative Republicans, led many Washington correspondents to question the depth of Kennedy's liberalism.

The actual need for some type of criminal-code reform bill was widely acknowledged and not at issue with any of the protesting groups. As Kennedy and many others pointed out, over 3000 criminal laws exist on the books with no standardized definitions or logical conditions. Offenses are scattered throughout all fifty titles of the criminal code, and at least eighty separate theft offenses and seventy counterfeiting and forgery offenses are listed in vague or confusing terms. Approximately eighty different words are used to describe an offender's state of mind during a crime, ranging from "lascivious" to "corrupt." Long-outdated laws still remain in the code. One such law makes it a crime to detain a government carrier pigeon, another to seduce a female passenger on a steamship. A third law prohibits anyone from "impairing the military effectiveness by a false statement" and was used to harass war protesters during the First World War.

Kennedy's team set about reforming the old criminal-code bills and outlining a new proposal in 1975. They consolidated many of the old laws, eliminated scores of them, and tried to streamline the code. The main thrust of the reform was to set standards for sentencing. Kennedy commented on the problem: "One offender may receive a sentence of probation, while another, convicted of the very same crime and possessing a comparable criminal history, may be sentenced to a lengthy term of imprisonment. Even two such offenders who are sentenced to similar terms of imprisonment may become subject to widely differing prison release dates: one may be paroled after serving only a small portion of his sentence while the other may be denied parole indefinitely." The new code provides federal judges with guidelines and review procedures for sentencing. One of the more regressive aspects of the code relates to the definition of the purpose of sentences, which is "deterrence, incarceration, punishment, and to a more limited extent, rehabilitation." The bill creates a sentencing committee "to develop a system of guidelines and policy statements designed to reduce sentencing disparity and uncertainty and provide more rational and determinate sentencing procedures." The guilty would be given definite prison sentences and the parole system would be abolished.

"The sentence imposed will be the sentence served . . . The offender, the victim and society all will know at the time of the initial sentencing decision what the prison release date will be."

The new system was intended to be more equitable, since wide disparities in sentencing would be eliminated. Determinate sentences and the absence of the possibility for parole aimed at having a deterrent effect because offenders would know precisely what the consequences of a particular crime would be. But it is a questionable assumption, for the passion or the need that usually underlies a criminal act has greater force than the knowledge that in some distant future the offender is likely to receive seven years in prison rather than five. Among the more controversial aspects of the bill is the abolition of parole, which many criminologists believe would undermine the motivation for rehabilitation.

The reorganization, nevertheless, would introduce much consistency into the criminal code. For example, each of the statutes on arson, the destruction of property, forgery, counterfeiting, perjury, false statements, theft, and fraud would be consolidated, which in itself would be a substantial achievement. The eighty definitions of the offender's mental state would be reduced to four — intentional, knowing, reckless, and negligent. A new law on rape would no longer require painful and often impossible corroboration of a victim's testimony. Possession of eavesdropping devices intended for illegal use would be prohibited. Certain civil rights laws would be expanded, including one provision that would outlaw discrimination on the basis of sex as well as race, color, and religion.

Many revisions were made to appease the civil rights groups and to consolidate the original massive and complicated earlier bill from 700 pages down to 400. The new act eliminated a section making it an offense to fail to obey a public safety order. It also dropped the crime of solicitation in one version of the bill and limited it in another, as well as dropping the crime of making a false oral statement in one version and making the provision in another that knowledge as to falsity was necessary. Parts of the bill permitting all crimes to be prosecuted as "attempts" and making it a new federal offense to "endeavor to persuade" someone to commit a crime were narrowed.

The American Civil Liberties Union was not satisfied with these revisions, though they described the bill as a "move toward striking a reasonable balance between law enforcement and civil liberties." Witnesses at the hearings on the bill asserted that they supported criminal-code reform in general but were disturbed about "the history of that process," and they advised a more cautious approach. Their objections to the bill were far more numerous than those already noted. But ACLU spokesmen were most disturbed by the provisions that dealt with sentencing, the core of the bill. "There is no coherent and consistent standard for the disposition of federal offenders. The system for guiding judicial discretion is inadequate. The bills do not emphasize alternative sentencing to incarceration. Finally, by abolishing parole and good time the bills close the safety valves of the present system and risk even longer periods of incarceration than under current law."

Ralph Nader, who is often far-sighted and constructive because he relates such problems to the economic base of the society, accused Kennedy of accepting compromises that resulted in ". . . a serious weakening of the proposals in the legislation to curb economic crimes, notwithstanding the almost daily publicized corporate crime epidemic sweeping the country." Nader's criticism raises serious questions about Kennedy's failure to press for legislation that does deal rigorously with the economic crimes perpetrated by businesses and multinational corporations. It suggests either that he does not foresee large-scale corporate crime transforming "free" markets into controlled markets, or that he is unwilling to make more enemies in the business community.

Kennedy never confronted Nader's criticism directly, but he tried to reassure others skeptical of the bill that further problems would be dealt with as he incorporated more revisions. Concerning freedom of the press, Kennedy reassured media representatives that "gag orders" limiting the activities of reporters prior to publication would be prohibited. In an address before newspapermen and magazine editors, he turned to the question of freedom of the press.

> I pledge to you, as Chairman of the Senate Judiciary Committee, that from whatever source the attack may come, I shall do everything in my power to protect the rights of the men and the women of the press. No reporter should go to jail for defending the First Amendment. No editor should be forced to take a lie detector test at the whim of a disgruntled plaintiff in a suit. No publisher should be the victim of large fines for defending his editors and reporters on his basic right to publish. If the Supreme Court drops the ball on issues like these, it is up to Congress and this administration to pick it up.

Kennedy avoided explosive issues with moral content, such as gun control and the death penalty, another pragmatic political move in an election year. On the subject of marijuana, possession of one ounce or less was defined as a nonarrestable infraction. But even on this count, Kennedy was criticized by representatives of the National Organization for the Reform of Marijuana Laws (NORML), who referred to the provision as a mere "token victory." The Kennedy clause on marijuana maintains the concept of "limited privacy," they said, because it permits an officer to search for marijuana and issue a ticket for possession. NORML wanted a more progressive law that would completely eliminate the offense of possession, but Kennedy refused to jeopardize his reputation by negotiating further on the issue.

Kennedy's liberal supporters have been disappointed and suspicious of his support for what they perceived as regressive and conservative aspects in the criminal-code revision. But this disappointment largely results from unrealistic expectations, since the realities of American politics and Kennedy's record demonstrate his history of playing both liberal ideologue and pragmatic moderate. As a candidate for the presidency, he will inevitably consider his own political survival first and foremost. He is courting many major constituencies, and the law and order constituency that Nixon helped to enhance years ago is particularly large now in America's major cities. It is one that Kennedy cannot afford to lose.

In sum, Kennedy demonstrates that he is a professional politician and not a moralist. He works within a system of incremental change and is unwilling to advance grandiose programs for social change if they transcend the boundaries of America's traditional liberalism and threaten electoral victories. The thrust of Kennedy's political career is liberal, but this has never prevented him from compromising or even assuming a conservative posture when it was politically expedient or "necessary" to do so. The most significant post that Kennedy has held thus far, the chairmanship of the Senate Judiciary Committee, demonstrates that his political activity and his followers' perceptions of his image have little to do with each other.

6

Foreign Policy and Defense: The Public Image

FOREIGN POLICY has become the dominant concern in presidential campaigns during the past decade. Despite spiraling inflation and serious energy problems, the people of the United States have become painfully aware of the fact that very few internal problems originate exclusively at home or can be solved there without reference to the international context of American politics. The interdependence among nations is so profound and so obvious that the American public, despite a yearning for isolationism, realizes it can no longer ignore what happens in countries such as Vietnam, Israel, Iran, or Afghanistan. Nostalgia for the simpler and less turbulent periods when isolationism or American power went unchallenged is no longer conceivable.

Television has had much to do with the international education of the American public. Today the networks cover even the most remote corners of the globe, and scenes from a riot in Pakistan or a revolution in El Salvador can be transmitted to homes in Dayton and Tallahassee the same day. But a two-minute spot on the news or a fifteen-minute special merely scratches the surface of events in other lands, and it is left to commentators and politicians, most particularly the President, to impart ideas and theories about those events to the public. The spontaneous character of international outbursts literally forces the people of the United States to realize that disturbances in the policies and the economies of other nations may be closely linked to those of their neighbors as well as to the superpowers. The international character of multinational corporations, cartels, and political coups will certainly affect the everyday lives, and possibly even the voting patterns, of large numbers of people. Public-opinion data have indicated recently that the traditional chauvinism that has characterized the American people, the view that the United States is the center and most important element in the free world, is slowly changing.

Foreign-policy debates among candidates and the growing awareness of interdependence among nations have profoundly affected the very nature of presidential campaigns. Candidates are now expected to demonstrate superior aplomb, savvy, and skill in the handling of foreign affairs before their audiences. International relations is now the primary forum in which the public image of presidential candidates is made or broken. Before the events in Iran, for example, President Carter trailed Edward Kennedy by a margin of two to one in the public-opinion polls. But in one of the most dramatic reversals in American political history, Carter was ahead of Kennedy by a margin of two to one within three months. Iran presented Carter with an opportunity to revoke his previous image as a weak President and display his authority on a volatile issue, so that the electorate began to perceive him as a serious and substantial leader on foreign affairs. The seizure of American hostages evoked such an outburst of patriotism that Carter was hardly criticized for causing the crisis by permitting the shah of Iran to enter the United States in the first place. The Iranian crisis is a prime example of the way in which spontaneous events abroad can seriously alter the public image of a politician, at least in the short run.

Candidates and political opponents may criticize each other's positions on specific international crises, particularly when the press is on hand to cover them. But each crisis is different, has its own set of circumstances, and calls for unprecedented decisions to be made by the chief executive, which makes a more complete understanding of the candidates' overall world vision imperative. The making of foreign policy is a far graver matter than the reaction to isolated events. It precludes the more superficial image and exposure that events may engender because it demonstrates the leader's ability to analyze a number of world events and to synthesize a coherent, overall pattern and direction from them. The formulation of a well-defined foreign policy is necessary to give a nation confidence in its role in the world, build the respect it seeks abroad, inspire confidence in other countries, and prevent needless crises that may arise largely from misunderstandings. "Leadership" is an important component in the successful execution of foreign policy.

Though there may be only slight differences on specific foreign-policy issues between President Carter and Edward Kennedy, the two candidates speak from very different forums, with vastly different styles and backgrounds. An incumbent President is judged on the basis of his record and may maximize his support and appear "presidential" by using the symbols and mantle of authority. He can instantly command the top political forum in the country as the spokesman for the United States on foreign policy, whereas the achievements of a senator or a congressman are likely to go unnoticed. In matters of foreign policy, the challenger can only prosper by the President's ineptitude. The onus is therefore on the challenger to separate himself from the President's policies and draw attention to the differences between his and the chief executive's global perspectives.

Even if the events in Iran had not occurred during the presidential campaign, Kennedy would have had a difficult time distinguishing his general foreign-policy outlook from that of the President. Neither Carter nor Kennedy takes issue with the virtues of American capitalism or the need to pursue a foreign policy favorably disposed to American business interests. Both believe in coexistence with the Soviet bloc, extol the virtues of "free enterprise," and deplore any form of "socialism" in America. The goal of both has been to foster American interests abroad and to persuade as many nations as possible that the American sphere of influence is more rewarding than the Soviet. Neither candidate has suggested means different from the other's for accomplishing these goals.

Style is what has set the two apart most distinctly. Before the crisis in Iran, President Carter seemed weak and unattractive behind the podium, a condition that image makers were unable to alter. Kennedy, on the other hand, had a certain flourish and vigor in public performances and could make his positions sound fresh and convincing, even if they were ill defined and unspecific. But beyond the disparity in styles and minor differences over the methods they would pursue to implement American foreign policy, Kennedy and Carter are in fundamental agreement about the goals that policy must serve.

Kennedy prefers to stress the fact that he has been

familiar with international issues for years and has more experience with policy making in the upper house, which provides advice and consent on treaties to the chief executive. Ever since he became a presidential candidate, Kennedy has been unable to involve the incumbent President in political debate on foreign affairs. Leadership is his issue, in foreign affairs as in domestic, and Kennedy is attempting to prove his superior skills over Carter's in three major areas: his capacity to be a strong and vigorous leader in foreign affairs, his expertise in developing a coherent foreign policy, and his ability to maintain firm control over the foreign-policy establishment.

*

Jimmy Carter's leadership in foreign affairs has been the subject of attack from the right and from the left, both at home and abroad. He has been criticized for frequent shifts or delays in implementing his foreign policies, which, many say, has helped to destabilize allies and adversaries alike and contribute to the decline of American prestige and influence abroad. Kennedy criticized him in particular for "allowing a proliferation of different voices to speak for the administration in foreign policy questions," for ignoring the needs of many allies and Third World countries, and for repeatedly reversing himself. For example, Kennedy noted that after Carter appointed Andrew Young and sent him to numerous African countries to pursue improved relations there, he allowed Young to be forced out of the administration and later alienated many friendly African leaders by sending arms and aid to the autocratic king of Morocco, who was fighting a war to take over the mineral-rich Spanish Sahara. He asserts that Carter reversed his original decision not to shelter the shah, his pledge not to sell arms to Turkey, and even his hard-line attitude toward Cuba when Soviet troops were discovered there, which Andrew Young said "was like shooting a cannon at a rat." (Young went on to say, "It's nonsense for us to be so obsessed with Cuba and Fidel Castro. He's a nuisance and that's how we should treat him . . . but instead we've built Castro up into a bogeyman.")

America's allies in Europe and elsewhere in the world have expressed bewilderment at one time or another at the unstructured and erratic character of American foreign policy under President Carter. Kennedy has capitalized on this discontent by citing their criticisms of the President. One report from a *New York Times* correspondent in Moscow, for example, claimed that the Soviets perceive most of Carter's foreign-policy problems to be of his own making. The President, Pravda noted, argued that the presence of Soviet troops in Cuba should not be cause for delaying the passage of SALT II, yet by increasing U.S. military forces in the Caribbean and engaging in a series of mock assaults, the President transformed the incident into a potential crisis and jeopardized the passage of the treaty. In reference to the President's address on the Soviet troops in Cuba, a Soviet official remarked: "There were sober-minded passages in the speech, maybe representing the Vance school, and there were others, probably written by Brzezinski, accusing us and the Cubans of aggressive actions all over the world. For two and a half years, there has been no real United States strategy. There are conflicting impulses. And because America is temporarily paralyzed in foreign policy, we're trying to do our best in a not very good situation."

Kennedy's position as a nonincumbent candidate unbounded by the constraints of the presidency allows him to make bold and noble promises while accusing the administration of multiple errors. It is one of the advantages of being the challenger who can be held accountable for nothing. He is aided by charges that issue from many other sectors, such as the editorial in a Hong Kong daily that said, "Carter has shown himself to be out of his depth in the White House," or one in a Rome newspaper that claimed, "the campaign will be tough, wearing and nasty, but . . . with Kennedy in the field . . . American politics has been jolted out of an apathy that has left the nation's problems unsolved." Columnists at home have said that Carter epitomizes "the indecisiveness and listlessness of the nation as a whole." So Kennedy chose to attack these aspects of Carter's presidency and lamented the "drifting" nature of the administration's foreign policies. He promises that if he is elected, he will enact a consistent and active foreign policy instead of merely "reacting" to crises that occur elsewhere in the world. While he berates Carter for general failings in overall foreign-policy making, he offers his character and personality to rectify the "crisis of leadership." But actually speaking in more specific terms has been virtually impossible. Kennedy, as challenger, desperately searches for issues on which to differ with the President and is experiencing trouble doing so on foreign policy primarily because there are very few issues on which they diverge, and because Iran and Afghanistan have pre-empted the foreign-policy debate for some time. Carter and Kennedy are very obviously members of the same wing of the Democratic party.

A number of analysts in and out of the administration lamented that when Andrew Young left, so did the hope for a resurgent post-Vietnam idealism in American foreign policy. Kennedy has tried to fill the void and reignite that enthusiasm, speaking in platitudes about the "native energies

of the American people" and the need for more firm leadership in the country and a redefinition of America's role in
the world today. But candidate Carter said many of the
same things when he was campaigning in 1976 about increasing initiatives to foreign neighbors and bringing a
new morality to foreign policy. As President, he found himself considerably restrained from implementing such
ideals, given the constraints of the office and the nature of
the system he was attempting to control. Kennedy, who is
already down-playing his "progressive" record in the Senate to reassure the more conservative constituents in his
audiences, might also find it very difficult to implement his
broad ideas.

He has made much of the fact that his experience in
foreign affairs is greater than Carter's. He has traveled
abroad since he was a child and lived in England as the son
of the ambassador, and he was received in many countries
as the emissary of President John Kennedy. According to
his staffers, the countries not yet visited in person by Kennedy are nevertheless familiar to him, since their leaders
often ask to meet with him while visiting Washington on
official business. Although he has never visited any sub-
Saharan African countries, he knows Kenneth Kaundra of
Zambia and Julius Nyerere of Tanzania personally. He met
the Sandinista leaders of Nicaragua before the administration would receive them, and his staff representatives have
met with Fidel Castro to prepare the ground for a future
meeting. He has visited many Latin American countries
and toured those in the Middle East and Asia, largely in
connection with his work on the Refugees Subcommittee.
His international contacts are impressive, and he has con-
ferred with President Valéry Giscard d'Estaing of France,
Willy Brandt of West Germany, and numerous Labour

leaders in Great Britain. He was allowed record-long meetings with Soviet President Leonid Brezhnev, who is said to have a high regard for Kennedy and met with him for four hours during a visit to Moscow in 1974 and for two hours in 1978. These are advantages that Carter did not have when he was first campaigning for the presidency, and Kennedy can cite them whenever Carter's inexperience is blamed for the President's inability to sound a firm note on foreign policy and for his having appointed people to top advisory positions who were unable to work together.

Kennedy's advisors like to stress the fact that many foreign leaders seek out the senator because of his reputation when they come to Washington. On the basis of his long record of Senate initiatives and votes, they compare his deeper commitment, as opposed to Carter's, on popular issues such as "human rights" and improved relations with Third World countries. Kennedy has tried to set his world vision apart by talking about greater American participation in the global community in more equitable relationships with other countries. He suggests that closer coordination of U.S. economic policies with those of other industrialized nations would solve numerous domestic problems. He claims to be more interested in the trade and energy needs of the Third World countries, and advocates tolerant and friendly relations with both the Soviet Union and China without playing one off against the other. The specifics for all of his ideas, however, are still only vaguely outlined and not radically different from Carter's. Even the issue of defense spending, on which Carter sought to separate himself from Kennedy by saying, "I would be in favor of much stronger defense commitments," brought them closer together when Kennedy agreed in 1979 to support the administration's first request for a 3 percent increase in the defense budget. But President Carter discovered that his popularity increased dramatically when he took a harder line on defense and the resurgence of American authority abroad, and though Kennedy does not take issue with this, he focuses his attacks on Carter's "leadership" and offers his own force and idealism as alternatives.

Kennedy's leadership on international issues in the Senate is uneven. He has chaired the Subcommittee on Refugees for twelve years and has customarily spoken out on foreign affairs from that forum, since he does not serve on the Foreign Relations Committee or the Armed Services Committee. A book that he wrote in 1968, *Decisions for a Decade,* dealt mainly with foreign policy, and he sponsored another book on defense policy, leading the fight against the ABM system in 1969. He has sponsored numerous amendments on international topics and lobbied in favor of SALT Treaties I and II, the Panama Canal Treaty, the cessation of U.S. aid to forces fighting the civil war in Angola, and normalization of relations with China, Vietnam, and Cuba. He has courageously criticized those regimes, allegedly "friendly" to the United States, that violate human rights, and he has granted audiences to critics of those regimes. But most of the positions on foreign policy taken by Kennedy during the first three years of the Carter administration were consonant with the President's positions. Disagreement between Carter and Kennedy on the defense budget amounted to only 1½ percent in 1979. Kennedy opposed Carter on construction of the MX and cruise missiles, the decision to sell advanced weapons to Middle East countries, and the resumption of aid to Turkey.

Kennedy had actually worked with Carter to help lobby for many of his international initiatives before the start of the campaign. When he declared his candidacy, however,

Kennedy tried to distance himself from the President, criticized the lack of leadership and respect for the United States, and pointed to his own record and reputation as proof of his superior abilities. As a nonincumbent candidate, his platitudes can be more idealistic and daring than the President's, and thus he applies stricter standards to countries that violate human rights, preaches more understanding of so-called hostile countries, and insists on more-egalitarian relations with Third World countries and the dissemination of more foreign aid for purposes other than political gain. But even as the campaign wears on, these messages have been moderated to accommodate American moods. As the nation shifts toward a more hardline approach to "adversaries" and a strengthening of defense commitments, so does Kennedy. If elected President, a proven pragmatist like Kennedy may eventually become as accommodating as the President he now opposes. In lieu of the recent crises in other parts of the world and Kennedy's proximity to most of Carter's foreign policies, he continues to proffer assurances of his force, drive, and idealism for the leadership void.

*

Kennedy repeatedly promises that he would formulate a more coherent and unified foreign policy if he becomes President. Given the scores of speeches on international topics he has delivered over the years and the innumerable press releases on his positions and his Senate votes, his policies are well developed and clearly delineated. To audiences that adhere to liberal views, he has been more vocal than Carter in the past in eschewing the attitude that the United States must police the globe to counter the "communist menace." Instead of dividing the world into dual "Cold War" spheres of interest, with the United States leading the free world and the Soviet Union dominating its satellites, he claims to perceive the global situation as far more complex and interdependent. The Soviet Union is seen by him to be in a position similar to the United States, constrained by numerous economic and political forces that dramatically limit its freedom of action. In contrast to other American politicians, Kennedy views the "communist threat" as overstated and not directly detrimental to the United States. He argues that most countries are concerned primarily about their own sovereignty and survival, and that the United States should not ". . . assume that its national interest is threatened because an insurgent movement adopts the 'Communist' or 'revolutionary' rubric. On a continent as poor as Asia, the rhetoric of Marxism has considerable appeal . . . But we should remember that Communism in the sense of an extension of Russian and Chinese power is an offense to Asian revolution, for it conflicts with the most powerful force in Asia today: nationalism." Kennedy, however, never defined his terms and did not attempt to explain how and why these forces conflicted. Like so many of his public statements, this pronouncement has the ring of liberalism and anti-imperialism without coming to grips with the interplay of these complex forces. Kennedy's political rhetoric is that of a liberal reformer who supports humanistic enterprises in the Third World and is skeptical of the more militant ideologies of Cold Warriors; but he makes no attempt to relate the purpose of American foreign policy to the protection and advancement of American economic interests. American foreign policy is rarely examined in terms of self-interest, although that of the Soviet Union and China is invariably portrayed in terms of economic and political power struggles. There are in Kennedy's approach to foreign relations undertones of the doctrine of Manifest Destiny, the view that the United States is the bastion of liberty obligated to extend its doctrine of representative government and free enterprise to the rest of the world. Although it is not a prime thrust of his view, it is an ever-present assumption.

For example, Kennedy never portrays "liberal" efforts to aid the development of the Third World as an integral part of the American effort to dominate the economy of these nations and safeguard U.S. interests. He would hardly be in favor of initiatives within those countries to alter the existing power structure along more radical lines, and therefore his analysis of American foreign policy in these areas, like Carter's, is somewhat superficial and concerned primarily with the maintenance of the status quo.

Kennedy's well-publicized positions on international issues are occasionally contradictory. In 1968, for example, he wrote sympathetically of nationalist movements abroad: "I don't think the record shows [the Soviets] have been successful [in Africa]. I fundamentally believe that in thirty or forty years, no matter what the great powers do, the Africans are going to live in African countries with African solutions. They are not going to trade one colonialism for another." In a speech before the Council on Foreign Relations in 1979, he advanced a less controversial argument, suggesting that the United States should compete with the Soviet Union and China for the allegiance of Third World countries. He argued that had the United States moved to normalize relations with Vietnam, that country might not have concluded a new alliance with the Soviet Union and would have limited its objectives in Cambodia. Also that year, Kennedy revived a touch of the Cold Warrior rhetoric — possibly because he sensed that the mood of the country was shifting to the right — when he presented the interests of the United States and the Soviet Union as being in direct and immediate opposition. Referring to the SALT II Treaty in a speech at Boston University, Kennedy argued that passage of the treaty "will certainly not change the fact that the United States and the Soviet Union are in fundamental and direct confrontation in both our political life and our economic systems. Only the basic instinct to survive appears to have prevented actual military confrontation and nuclear disaster so far. As an unabashed partisan of our own political and economic system, I am confident that we will prevail, whether through nonmilitary competition or through peaceful cooperation." It is probably not coincidental that this statement by Kennedy occurred during a period when he was charged with being "soft" on the Soviet Union because he was a vigorous supporter of SALT II.

Despite Kennedy's reference to the rights of Third World people and the need for building new and creative relationships with other countries, his position is basically the same as that of Carter and the more liberal Republican contenders. Neither Kennedy nor Carter considers a substantial alteration of the international status quo. Neither considers an actual restructuring of international economic relations or the premises upon which our foreign policy is based.

The makers of American foreign policy are fond of devoting verbal attention to the problems of Third World countries, although Carter's foreign policy suggests that verbal concern is belied by the practicalities of that policy and by financial interests. The contribution of the United States in official development assistance to Third World countries, for example, has been declining for the past decade, and

Carter has done nothing to reverse this trend. The U.S. contribution is second lowest of all Western industrial nations, less than that of Sweden, the Netherlands, France, Britain, and Germany, measured as a percentage of the GNP. The United States continues to attach restrictions to its contributions through the World Bank and through trade agreements. Other countries have found this less than generous and the economist Robert Lekachman, by no means a radical, analyzed the situation in terms that neither Kennedy nor Carter is willing to do:

> Aside from its grant to international agencies, the United States gives aid in pursuit of geopolitical aims rather than in recognition of development needs. For example, the foreign aid funding bill for fiscal 1980 passed by the Senate earmarked for the Middle East eighty-five percent of the proposed economic aid; [also,] the Federal Reserve's savage assault on credit availability will dramatically increase the cost of new or renewed loans to poor countries and inevitably diminish the total flow of loans to them.

Kennedy neither highlights the geopolitical character of our support of Third World countries, nor does he outline specific plans designed to ease their economic problems. Carter's position is equally uncritical of the forces of self-interest, which he well knows delimit the extent of our humanism.

Kennedy's record, however, does illustrate a long-standing concern for the disadvantaged of Third World countries. Some critics assert that Kennedy's position is simply evidence of classic liberal guilt, but the facts of his support stand for themselves. When Kennedy and his aides were drafting a national health plan for the United States, they included a plan for health research to help poor countries. Kennedy also proposed legislation that would require

American banks to disclose any loans made to foreign governments whose aid had been curtailed because of human rights violations. Numerous American banks have filled the credit gap and undercut U.S. foreign policy when the President had cut off assistance.

Morton Kondracke of the *New Republic* wrote: "Kennedy deserves credit for consistent concern about the world's refugees, its starving and homeless people. Carter, like other politicians, has shown his compassion about the same time that the world's television networks decide to turn their attention to boat people or Cambodians. Kennedy has been holding hearings, sending study missions and beating drums for refugee aid since the mid-1960s." Whatever the political or personal motivations for his actions in this area, they have benefited large numbers of people.

He stepped forward on crucial "liberal" issues early in his career, and as chairman of the Subcommittee on Refugees, he held numerous hearings and developed programs to ease the plight of refugees from the Vietnam War. In 1979 he used his influence and experience to publicize the plight of the "boat people" in Vietnam and the homeless refugees in Cambodia. He sponsored the bill that raised the number of refugees permitted to enter the United States each year from 17,400 to 50,000 and repeatedly criticized Carter for doing too little too late for the famine victims. In lamenting the barbarity of Pol Pot's government in Cambodia, he did admit that "Cambodia is on our conscience . . . we cannot escape the moral consequences of our actions during the Vietnam War, which helped to launch the descent into hell of that once beautiful and peaceful land." He authored several amendments to allocate millions of dollars for Cambodian refugees in Vietnam and elsewhere, to be channeled through the United Nations.

Kennedy has favored the normalization of relations with Vietnam since 1975. The government of Vietnam on occasion sends messages to the U.S. government through Kennedy or Senator George McGovern, since there are no official ties between the two countries. In late 1975, Vietnam's foreign minister sent a letter to Kennedy thanking him for supporting normalization and reconstruction assistance for Vietnam, and informed him that Vietnam would return the bodies of two American servicemen who had died there. In 1976 Kennedy's Subcommittee on Refugees praised the new economic zones in Vietnam in a staff report; also that year, the Vietnamese embassy in Paris cabled Kennedy that American citizens would be authorized to leave the southern part of Vietnam. Premier Pham Van Dong sent a letter to Kennedy in 1978 indicating a willingness to pursue diplomatic relations with the United States without the precondition that the United States make reparations payments to Vietnam. Kennedy refrained from criticizing the Vietnamese government recently when thousands of boat people left the country.

Beginning in 1966, Kennedy also favored American recognition of China, long before it was fashionable to do so. At first he insisted that relations with Taiwan should not be sacrificed for recognition but later he came to oppose adamantly a two-China approach. In the late sixties he proposed a seven-point plan to enhance U.S.-Chinese relations, open talks for diplomatic ties, withdraw U.S. opposition to Chinese entry into the United Nations, and exchange trade, science, and cultural delegations. In *Decisions for a Decade,* he wrote: "Is the 'China Peril' concept a reality on which to base a foreign policy, as opposed to a last-ditch device to scare Americans into backing a policy that has lost its other justifications?" He lobbied heavily to support the

Carter administration's effort to open diplomatic relations with China in 1979, but is averse to cooperating more closely with the Chinese at the expense of relations with the Soviets. He visited China with his family in 1978, met with Vice-Premier Deng Xiaoping and other officials, and toured a number of factories and health facilities.

Because Kennedy has been such a strong supporter of detente with the Soviet Union, he has been accused of being "soft" on the Soviets and naive about their global intentions. He believes that "pursuit of detente and human rights is too serious an imperative for us to be sidetracked into righteous posturing and rhetoric which set back either or both of these objectives," and that Americans should recognize "the likelihood that the Soviet leadership feels beset by an unprecedented number of internal and external challenges." Critics on the right have asserted that it is dangerous that he does not view the overall objectives of the Soviet Union as intrinsically hostile. But others, like Morton Kondracke of the *New Republic*, note that "he thinks that the first foreign policy priority of a U.S. President should be to prevent World War III, and he thinks that Soviet leaders, having experienced the ravages of World War II, share that aim." He favors increased trade and cultural ties to help ease tensions with the Soviets and gave his unqualified support to SALT II as it faced a hostile Senate. Being somewhat familiar and friendly with Soviet leaders since his visits to Moscow in 1974 and 1978, he seems less suspicious of Soviet aims around the world than other presidential candidates.

Kennedy returned from the 1978 trip with a list of Jewish families (relatives of his constituents) who the Soviets had agreed could emigrate from the country; and he met with dissidents, including Andrei Sakharov and told him that the two countries should proceed with arms control agreements; this places him in complete accord with President Carter.

Kennedy was such an outspoken critic of several Latin American dictators that Somoza had placed his name on a list of "potential enemies of the government of Nicaragua" in 1975. He sponsored an amendment with Senator Frank Church in 1978 to cut off aid to Somoza, then wrote a letter with a number of other senators to President Carter, urging him to pressure Somoza to step down. He introduced the first amendment to cut off aid to the repressive military regime in Chile in 1973, and worked to allow 26,000 Chilean refugees who were attempting to flee that regime into the United States (over Henry Kissinger's opposition). He opposed Kissinger's wishes to resume military aid to Chile in 1975, publicized the names of victims who have been tortured or have "disappeared" there, and sharply criticized the Chilean government's decision not to extradite Orlando Letelier's murderers to the United States for trial (as did President Carter).

Kennedy has always granted audiences to those lobbyists for refugees, dissidents, and families of torture victims who were not received by the administration (particularly when Kissinger was secretary of state) and cooperates with them in sponsoring amendments for their causes. His outspoken positions have made him immensely popular with the people of Latin America. Many government-run newspapers under the military dictatorships in Latin American countries print virulent attacks against him, which only serve to increase his popularity with people there, since most of them distrust the government news. His position on maintaining ties with "friendly" Latin nations that violate human rights is less compromising than Carter's has been, and he opposed the DeConcini Amendment to the Panama Canal Treaty, which sanctions the use of force by the United States to keep the canal open.

Kennedy also voices his plans for a more cohesive approach to Africa and cooperative efforts with African leaders on finding solutions to their problems, although he does not specify exactly how he intends to go about this. Like Carter, he has persistently opposed the apartheid governments in southern Africa and this has heightened his standing among black African leaders, but his motives for this opposition were diverse. Oil figured largely in influencing his foreign-policy outlines, and he argued in 1979 (as did the Carter administration) that U.S. economic sanctions against Zimbabwe/Rhodesia should not be lifted because such a move might "set back our political and economic interests throughout Africa, including those with Nigeria, which is our second largest supplier of oil." Reverting to a useful piece of Cold War rhetoric, he warned that lifting the bans might "open the door wider to Cuban and Soviet involvement, further reducing the prospects for peace in southern Africa." He opposed an amendment (as did President Carter) put forward by Senators Moynihan of New York and Hayakawa of California to send observers to the elections in Zimbabwe/Rhodesia in early 1979, since such a move would give the elections — which he called unrepresentative — a certain legitimacy from the United States. He has said little about South Africa directly, but he voiced strong disapproval of Carter's decision to send military aid to King Hassan of Morocco.

Kennedy has cautiously towed the administration line on the Middle East, supporting the Camp David agreements between Israel and Egypt and opposing the inclusion of any Palestinian representatives in the peace talks. He often skirts the subject and is quick to assure the Israelis, along with the large numbers of Jewish voters in the United States, of his support. At the end of 1979, he called for an increase of $350 million to the $1.8-billion aid package pledged annually to Israel, purportedly to offset inflation. In effect, he hopes to capitalize on the Jewish disaffection with Carter, manifested ever since the President adopted a tougher line toward Israel in his attempt to court the Arabs.

Speaking on Israeli television during a visit there in 1979, he stressed his "strong commitment to Israel, to its security, to defensible borders, to its economic strength and vitality." In another speech he reiterated that "there should be no direct or even indirect talks with the PLO, certainly until there's a recognition among the leadership of that organization of Israel's right to exist in peace."

In regard to U.S. policies on Iran, Kennedy held back his criticisms for quite some time. He denounced the shah's regime several times during the monarch's reign, even though he had visited the shah in 1975, at which time he merely "questioned the wisdom" of the Iranian arms buildup. When the hostages were taken in Teheran, he said nothing and quietly supported the administration's decision to move with caution and attempt to conduct negotiations. Kennedy grew increasingly frustrated when the situation allowed Carter to monopolize the news media and finally voiced the opinion that the shah's regime was "one of the most violent in the history of mankind." He implied by the statement that Carter had made an error in permitting the shah to enter the country and that the Iranian people had legitimate grievances against the monarch. Coming either before the seizure or after the safe release of the hostages, it would have been a fair and challenging criticism; but the poor timing of his remarks cost him dearly.

His criticism of other repressive dictators has been

forthright but has generally caused less trouble for him. He pressed the administration to show displeasure with human rights violations by the late South Korean President Park Chung Hee and issued public statements condemning the arrest of opposition figures like Kim Young Sam, again attempting to beat Carter onto the public record. Generals Videla of Argentina and Pinochet of Chile have been constant subjects of his scathing remarks.

Kennedy cosponsored the resolution in 1975 to cut off CIA funds to anticommunist rebels in Angola, insisting that the United States should stay out of another Vietnam-style civil war. He also proposed legislation that year to end U.S. restrictions against exports to Cuba, and has favored the opening of diplomatic relations with that country to defuse a major source of Soviet-American tension. Ever since Turkey overran parts of Cyprus in 1974, he has opposed the resumption of military aid to that country, although he does support provisions for economic aid and Foreign Military Sales (FMS) grants. As conditions to the resumption of aid, the senator has insisted that Turkey agree to permit its territory to be used for SALT verifications, that it proceed with discussions on terminating the military occupation of Cyprus, and that it allow Greece to return to NATO's military structure.

On European matters, Kennedy favors a peaceful solution to the problems in Northern Ireland and criticizes IRA "terrorist" activities, although he does support the eventual goals for reunification of the Republic of Ireland. He supports a united Europe with a strong Common Market and European Parliament, as does Carter, and he wants to see the European countries work more closely together on defense systems so that they might be less reliant on the United States. Like Carter, he holds that problems with inflation, energy scarcity, unemployment, and trade should be attacked jointly and that the United States can cooperate more closely with the Western Europeans. He has called on all the industrialized nations to loosen trade restrictions and straighten persistent imbalances in order to decrease inequitable trade policies that harm the underdeveloped nations. He is counting on the European Monetary System to help stabilize sharply fluctuating foreign-exchange rates.

His diatribes on expanding the North-South dialogue between rich and poor nations are almost indistinguishable from Carter's of 1976. But he has been active on those issues since the early seventies, advocating the de-emphasis of military and strategic ties with Third World countries and more stress on economic cooperation (to ensure their friendliness to American interests). He advised the revitalization of the East-West dialogue to defuse tension in Europe and enhance detente with the Soviet Union, until the Soviet invasion of Afghanistan, at which time he supported all the President's economic moves against the Soviets except the grain embargo. He believes that better economic and trade ties, such as extending most-favored-nation (MFN) status to the Soviet Union, would ensure friendly relations and possibly prevent a third world war. Advocating MFN status for Hungary and Rumania, he wants to attract Eastern European nations, with stronger economic ties as incentives.

On the subject of defense, Kennedy has always been an advocate of arms reductions. He supported SALT I and II on the condition that the United States have ample opportunities for verfication, and he opposed the attempts by Jackson and Moynihan to withhold treaty ratification until the Soviets ease their emigration restrictions. He warns that in the absence of a treaty, there is a grave danger of further arms escalations. During the campaign, however, he has spoken less of the need for arms limitation because the Soviet invasion of Afghanistan has fueled the public disposition for a more vigorous military posture by the United States. During the late fall of 1979, President Carter shifted his position on the defense budget in favor of substantially greater expenditures. Kennedy agreed to support an increase in the Pentagon budget of 3 percent after adjustments were made for inflation. But in his speech last December announcing his new resolution to boost the defense budget drastically, the President chose to side with the Cold Warriors on his staff who advocated a tougher stance toward "unfriendly" countries. Warning that the United States would intervene anywhere that "national interests" were threatened in the world with a Rapid Deployment Force, Carter repeatedly evoked fears of the Soviet "threat" at the end of 1979: "The steady buildup by the Soviets, and their growing inclination to rely on military power to exploit turbulent situations, call for a calm, deliberate and sustained American response . . . we are moving rapidly to counterbalance the growing ability of the Soviet Union, directly or through surrogates, to use its military power in Third World regions and we must be prepared to deal with hostile actions against our citizens or our vital interests from others as well."

Carter emphasized the need to increase defense spending at least 14 percent annually to counter the effects of inflation, which would mean annual expenditures of over $200 billion within five years. He intends to bolster and modernize the navy; deploy the MX blockbuster missile, which "will have the capability to attack a wide variety of Soviet military targets"; modernize ground forces; and build a fleet of CX cargo planes to carry marines for his Rapid Deployment Force.

Kennedy, on the other hand, has been eager to pursue means other than military to redress America's poor image in the Third World countries. He wants to see existing defense funds rechanneled so that new weapons systems and defensive capabilities would be explored. He opposed construction of the MX missile because of its costs and because of the alarm it might cause the Soviets. He opposed the B1 bomber (as did Carter), nuclear aircraft carriers, and the neutron bomb (for both financial and moral reasons, claiming that any bombs developed simply to destroy more people rather than targets are fundamentally wrong). But he has largely muffled his opposition to all systems currently under development during the campaign, and has yet to elaborate on preferred alternatives.

Apart from the issue of defense, Kennedy's foreign policies can be clearly seen as coinciding to a large extent with Carter's. His support for almost all of the President's foreign-policy initiatives over the last few years demonstrates that the two have few actual grounds of disagreement. Thus, when Kennedy refers to the coherent policy line he would formulate if elected, it appears that he is once again speaking more in terms of style than content.

*

When Kennedy claims that he could certainly maintain firm control over the foreign-policy establishment, he cites convincing evidence that President Carter has not been able to do so. Carter, he argues, has permitted a "proliferation of different voices to speak for the administration in foreign-policy questions." By contrast, the senator portrays a Kennedy administration as one that would have "a voice that's predictable and certain, that our allies could rely on and our adversaries would respect." During Carter's first three years in office, public attention was focused on his inexperience in foreign affairs and the conflicts among his major foreign-policy advisors. Columnists charged that the President's circle of Georgian advisors could deal with local and state politics or the management of campaigns, but they had proved inept at running the country.

Bickering among the President's staff and cabinet officers often made headlines before the Ayatollah Khomeini inadvertently resurrected Carter's image. Secretary of State Cyrus Vance and foreign-policy advisor Zbigniew Brzezinski were continually undercutting each other and competing for the President's ear, both seeking to emerge as the leading voice on foreign-policy matters. One high administration official charged that "President Carter's way of making decisions depends on who gets to him last. If it's Brzezinski rather than Vance, then Zbig's solution will be adopted." Columnist Jack Anderson recently aired a sharp memo sent from Vance to Brzezinski, after Brzezinski circulated a questionnaire to all U.S. ambassadors abroad requesting data on Cuban activities in their areas for use in a worldwide propaganda campaign. Vance wrote: "The continued U.S. diplomatic emphasis on the Cuban-Soviet relationship is counter-productive and particularly inappropriate at this time. The U.S. can best secure the cooperation of the Third World countries, both in the long run and during this crisis [in Iran] by recognizing that they have legitimate national concerns entirely apart from the U.S.-Soviet relationship." Anderson reported that Brzezinski's Cold War campaign continued nevertheless and has caused widespread revolt in the foreign-policy establishment.

Andrew Young was publicly chastised and frequently the victim of the White House cabal while he was Carter's U.S. ambassador to the United Nations. Three different men in three years have been sent to the Middle East as "trouble-shooters" to act as emissaries for the Carter peace proposals (one of the "experts," Robert Strauss, had no background or previous experience on Middle East issues). The cabinet shakeup and dismissals in the summer of 1979 further unsettled many foreign leaders and business executives. These men spent several years adjusting to Carter's administrative reshuffling, as they attempted to decipher policy lines and met new counterparts and learned how to deal with them. But when the Treasury and Commerce Department heads (among others) were dismissed and a new staff took over, past policies and precedents were flung aside and the working patterns that entwine our economy and government with those of other countries were further ruptured. With the Bert Lance affair early in his term and now a scandal surrounding his top advisor, Hamilton Jordan, Carter's image as an able administrator is poor.

Adroit administration is part of the reputation of the Kennedy machine. He seems to be more adept at coordinating his staffers than in spelling out his actual policy plans, and his staff has been largely responsible for manufacturing his activist profile. The top person advising him on foreign-policy matters is thirty-two-year-old Jan Kalicki, who earned a Ph.D. in International Relations from the London School of Economics specializing in Chinese-American relations. Kalicki spent several years in the State Department on the policy-planning staff, as well as two years at the U.S. Arms Control and Disarmament Agency. Apart from his staff, Kennedy has drawn on older, more experienced internationalists like Averell Harriman and Robert McNamara. These practices have led scholars and analysts to project that, at the very least, they would expect from a Kennedy presidency an almost Rooseveltian type of cabinet, with the appointment of one or two eminent Republicans along with his Democratic secretaries in an attempt to unite the country behind him. They suggest that he would probably insist on naming even the assistant and deputy secretaries under his cabinet secretaries so that uniformity and loyalty would characterize all his departments.

Carter has been criticized for allowing a larger number of patronage appointments at the department level. Some believe this resulted from the fact that the Georgians were unfamiliar with the pool of expertise available in universities and business. Professionals in the bureaucracy were much angered, particularly those in the State Department. While campaigning for the presidency, Carter wrote in *Why Not the Best*, "For many years in the State Department, we have chosen from among almost 16,000 applicants about 100 of our nation's finest young leaders to represent us in the international world. But we top this off with the disgraceful and counterproductive policy of appointing unqualified persons to major diplomatic posts as political payoffs. This must be stopped immediately." One of the assistant secretaries in the department recalled that the day Carter promised "to rely almost completely" on career foreign-service officers for the top State desks and ambassadorial posts abroad, then–Secretary of State Henry Kissinger walked into his 8:00 A.M. staff meeting and joked, "Well I see that Carter's just won the whole building!" But Carter just as quickly alienated many of them by naming political supporters rather than foreign-service officers to the top positions. Under Kissinger, every assistant secretary but one was a career foreign-service man, whereas under Vance (primarily due to Carter's urging) the number has dropped to less than half. As for ambassadors abroad, Carter's record is no better than Nixon's was, with approximately 62 percent of the ambassadorial posts filled by career foreign-service officers.

Opinions in other parts of the world on the desirability of a Kennedy presidency are as mixed as they are at home. The subject has evoked intense reactions everywhere, since his brother John's legend still thrives and Edward himself is no stranger in foreign capitals. In Western Europe, Kennedy receives sharply divided reviews. The French media treated Kennedy like a sure winner (according to *Washington Post* correspondents) and filled their magazines with features on "The Kennedy Myth." The West Germans are more skeptical of him, and the British press has carried harsh attacks on his character, referring to the scandals in his past. One British official said, "I have been struck by the virulence of criticism against Kennedy in the British press. In the less-informed press it deals with Chappaquiddick and Kennedy's morals; they seem to imply that history stopped at Chappaquiddick and say, 'He panicked there, so what's going to happen during an East-West crisis if he's President?' And on Northern Ireland he is seen as just another American politician trying to exploit the issue."

Officially, the British government regards his position on Northern Ireland as highly responsible, and embassy officials in Washington have dealt extensively with Kennedy on matters relating to the issue. One official explained that most Europeans, politicians included, do not really comprehend the American political system and have great difficulty in understanding why a Democratic President is unable to work with a Democratic Congress. Therefore they would not criticize Carter's leadership as being weak, and are skeptical that Kennedy's skills in managing bills in the Congress will necessarily mean he would make a better President. Though Margaret Thatcher's Conservative government might hedge at welcoming a Kennedy presidency because of his reputation as an advocate of social programs (at the expense of defense), Labour party officials would be more comfortable with him ideologically.

Kennedy has always received wide coverage in the Soviet press, particularly during his visits to Moscow in 1974 and 1978. The leadership there tends to view President Carter's top advisor, Zbigniew Brzezinski, as a Cold Warrior who is responsible for the decline in U.S.-Soviet relations. Many of them have expressed uncertainty about Carter's overall foreign policy and consider him incapable of helping America define its new role on the world stage. Partly for these reasons and partly because Brezhnev himself respects Kennedy, one official confided that the Soviets would welcome a Kennedy presidency, although they would still have major questions about a number of his positions. They maintain that he would adopt a coherent policy line that would enable them to know exactly what they were dealing with, and that he would assemble a competent and progressive cabinet to advise him.

Chinese officials are always reluctant to comment on American elections, but observers in Peking reported that the Chinese are leery of Kennedy's support for detente with the Soviets and for SALT II. During his visit to China in 1977, he spoke with Deng Xiaoping and visited a number of schools, health facilities, and homes. His foreign-policy advisor, Jan Kalicki, went to China in August 1979 to gather more information for Kennedy.

In most of the Third World countries, Kennedy is viewed as mythic primarily because he is a Kennedy and brother of the legendary President John. We noted earlier that Latin Americans tend to be as taken with Edward Kennedy as they were with JFK. For them, and the people of many other Third World countries, John Kennedy's charisma extends to Edward Kennedy. For the same reasons, many of the Arab peoples are said to adulate the Kennedys. The former President won the allegiance of many Arabs because of his charm and youth, and because he was perceived as a friend of the late Egyptian president and hero, Gamal Abdel Nasser. President Carter, on the other hand, is unpopular because he is perceived as being weak and disloyal to Arab causes. Upon assuming office, Carter pledged to work for a Palestinian homeland, but ultimately switched this position. He promised in October 1978 to work with the Soviets for peace in the Middle East but withdrew the offer when the Israelis protested. His decision to allow the shah into the United States did not endear him to devout Moslems.

Edward Kennedy, in contrast, perceived as part of the Kennedy myth, is assumed to be more influential than any other politician in Washington. Arab Africans dislike Carter for the reasons mentioned, and black Africans have even more reason. They were impressed by Andrew Young and delighted that an American administration was finally ready to turn a sympathetic ear to them. Carter, however, alienated many of his new supporters when Young resigned and the administration strengthened military ties with the king of Morocco.

The image of Edward Kennedy has been impressively propagated in Third World countries. But it is crucial for him in 1980 to be perceived at home as a vigorous leader

and an expert on international affairs. This has not occurred. Since the incidents in Iran and Afghanistan, the President, not Kennedy, has emerged as "the leader." Edward
Kennedy assumed that he could defeat Carter on the issues,
on inflation and energy, on unemployment and national
health. But "the issue" has become the character and morality of Edward Kennedy. Chappaquiddick, and the doubt
it casts on Kennedy and Camelot, is the issue for millions.

7

The Mystique Ends

THE WORLD IS made of dreams, and contrary to Karl Marx, the poor frequently love the rich and live vicariously through them.

The extensive Kennedy campaign apparatus of 1962, staffed by shrewd operatives whose activities were never curbed for lack of funds, would probably have mattered little if the candidate himself were not a man in whom the public could see substantial assets. And this brings us to the issue of the charisma of Edward Kennedy.

Prior to the events in Iran in late 1979 and early 1980, columnists and political commentators could not write about Edward Kennedy without speaking of the Kennedy charisma, the Kennedy mystique, the Camelot legend, all of which were taken for granted. The assumption of professional politicians and newspaper and television people was that Edward Kennedy would defeat Carter substantially, not, primarily, because Carter was perceived as ineffectual, but because Kennedy evoked a charismatic identification among his followers and displayed a unique set of attributes that made him so venerated and loved, so special and exciting that no opponent could possibly compete. Nine weeks after the embassy was attacked in Iran, the columnist, Mary McGrory, who covered the Iowa primary campaign, reported that "the thrill is gone from the Kennedy campaign in Iowa." McGrory explained succinctly what made this thrill evaporate. "When he first declared that he would make Iowa a test of strength, Kennedy was only running against Jimmy Carter. But since then he has acquired the ayatollah and Leonid Brezhnev as adversaries. His issues were to be energy and inflation. They have been buried under concern for international terrorism and aggression." Before the Iranian crisis, Edward Kennedy led the President in the polls by two to one; several weeks into the Iranian situation, the President led Edward Kennedy by a margin of two to one, a reversal so massive, in such a brief period, that it is unique in presidential poll taking. McGrory noted that ". . . the flame under the charisma has been turned so low that it seems almost to have gone out, and the motivation seems muffled."

Charisma is a term that newspapermen and television commentators like to play with. The word does have a mellifluous quality and is not part of the common linguistic coinage. "Charisma" has an exotic appeal as a concept. To members of the American media, the word connotes the candidate's ability to attract great crowds and generate and sustain an "electric" excitement, cheers, and applause. It means the evocation of a "Sinatra-like" sense of awe, a sense of being in the presence of a special person, a person whose presence calls forth screaming, whistling, stomping — silence or tumultuous applause. Responses of this kind are not common except to rock groups and Hollywood celebrities. What the media describes as charisma, however, is not what the concept means among scholars and theologians, whose preserve it was long before Walter Cronkite and James Reston heard of the term.

The concept was formulated by the master of modern sociology, Max Weber, and its meaning is very specific. Charisma refers ". . . to a certain quality of an individual personality by virtue of which he is set apart from ordinary men and treated as endowed with supernatural, superhuman, or at least specifically exceptional powers or qualities. These are such as are not accessible to the ordinary person, but are regarded as of divine origin or as exemplary, and on the basis of them, the individual is treated as a leader."

During the 1962 Senate campaign, one might think that Edward Kennedy actually possessed some of the attributes of charisma. There were the crowds and the yelling and screaming, the excitement was at times "electric," and the aura of celebrity was present. It was difficult to tell if this celebration was actually for John Fitzgerald Kennedy — whether Edward Kennedy was actually a surrogate, a minicharismatic figure who merely basked in the reflected charisma of the true star, or whether he was charismatic in his own right.

Even if one could sort out these possibilities, the fact remains that, primarily among the Irish, a sense of the royal was present. An elderly Irish ward politician who was close to Edward McCormack commented in 1962 on the nature of Edward Kennedy's appeal.

I honestly believe the Americans of Irish extraction look up to the Kennedys as royal blood . . . They like John Kennedy because he's Irish and Catholic and has taken them up a few steps socially . . . Everybody realizes and recognizes the Kennedys are all wealthy. Now, a lot of people say, "If I had a lot of money I'd be enjoying myself, I'd be over in the Riviera, I'd be cutting out coupons, but these people want to serve the public." And this is the great thing they have going for them. They are not ones to sit back and enjoy the money that they've inherited or compiled over the years; they want to do something useful. And this in the Irish makes them proud. I'm sure this is the basic thing among the Irish, to know the Kennedys is a social step upward. Everyone will tell you they've pictures of the President in their homes, these Irish people, Americans of Irish extraction. And they'll tell you, oh yes, I knew Rose Fitzgerald when she lived up in Wells Avenue. Or I knew Honey Fitz when he came out to speak at a communion breakfast fifteen years ago.

The political correspondent of the *Berkshire Eagle*, A. A. Michelson, a very astute observer of Massachusetts politics, adroitly put the issue. "There is sort of a princely effect in the Ted Kennedy campaign. In any dynasty the king is respected and obeyed, but everyone loves the prince and Ted Kennedy seems to have that attraction, wherever he goes."

This princely effect, this perception of royal blood, this Americanized charisma, is interesting because it is connected with the concept of noblesse oblige, a concept traditionally associated with nations that have had a feudal and a conservative tradition. Some of the Irish constituents are impressed by the fact that Edward Kennedy is "royal" and rich but wishes to serve the public. This, in itself, is taken as proof of his extraordinary life. The mix that feeds Edward Kennedy's alleged charisma is both bourgeois and conservative, thoroughly American, yet aristocratic. Perceptions of Kennedy in 1962 invariably contained three elements: that the candidate is from an enormously wealthy family, that the family is itself a First Family, and that the rich youngest son had in fact notified the citizens of Massachusetts that he intended to be a public servant. That wealth should be the backdrop of charisma is not surprising in bourgeois America, where status is rarely achieved on any other basis.

Greed may be the American way, and self-interest, but aristocratic service is attractive to Americans, perhaps because practitioners of noblesse oblige have transcended what Americans desire but feel is ignoble.

In a nation like the United States, which has no feudal inheritance, no hereditary aristocracy, no dukes, no earls or barons, how does one achieve such a status? The answer is, clearly through affluence. The status of the overwhelming majority of Americans is measured, by themselves and by others, in terms of wealth and wealth alone. The Kennedy money is, therefore, very appealing. But voters in 1962 also referred to the Kennedy family — the First Family — and to Kennedy's commitment to civic duty.

There is much to be learned about the nature of American political culture, and about the power and prestige of the Kennedy family, if one can properly sort out the meaning of this triad of duty, wealth, and family.

John Fitzgerald Kennedy, Edward Kennedy, and Robert Kennedy are not the only Americans whose rise to power was based upon a popular perception of their civic duty, their wealth, and the "royal" character of their family. The Kennedy brothers are part of a larger group of men who have entered public life throughout our history, men who, in the words of the fashion magazine, *Vogue,* may be called "beautiful people." Nelson Rockefeller was a "beautiful person," as are his Republican colleagues, Henry Cabot Lodge, John Lindsay, George Bush, and William Scranton. Their democratic counterparts include, in recent years, the governor of Massachusetts, Endicott Peabody; the distinguished mayors of Philadelphia, Richardson Dillworth and Joseph Clark; Senator Claiborne Pell of Rhode Island; Nelson Rockefeller's nephew, former governor of West Virginia; and his Uncle Winthrop, former governor of Arkansas. The Tafts of Cincinnati provided one President and the Roosevelts of New York supplied two. The appeal of such people to the American electorate, if properly understood, sheds light not only on the Kennedy mystique but also illuminates deeper currents in American politics.

The Kennedys are among those figures in American public life who could legitimately be called prestigious national celebrities, a rare political asset. For millions of Americans, the Kennedy brothers have "class" and produce an excitement beyond the norm. They associate with and are seen with poets, scholars, church leaders, socialites, beautiful women, and statesmen. Yet they can take off white tie and tails, compel presidents of steel companies to rescind price increases, invade Cuba, force the governor of Alabama to admit black students to public schools, and relentlessly pursue Jimmy Hoffa.

The "beautiful person," loves "the good things of life," yet he can rough it — climb mountains and trek through jungles as Teddy Roosevelt did. Such a person is elegant, yet willing to get his hands dirty. He is rich, yet works hard. He can drink imported wines or Coca-Cola. He travels in society, yet can be friendly with the man in the street. These patrician sons of wealthy and aristocratic families, with occasional exceptions, attend "proper" eastern private schools and Ivy League colleges, marry socially prominent debutantes, belong to the liberal wing of their party — be it Democratic or Republican — live in the very best part of town, summer in the "right places," speak with a broad *A*, and often ski. Their wives wear designer clothes, and their homes are photographed as examples of gracious but informal living. They are not quite American, yet they are very American. They symbolize two opposing, but fundamental, American ideals, aristocracy and equality. And this dual image is an enormous political advantage because the American people can project onto them their yearning for aristocracy and class and, simultaneously, their ideal of a democratic leader.

These men win elections, in part, because they are American ego-ideals and because they have the funds necessary to play big-time politics. Some also win because they are bright, reasonable, and energetic. The secret of their appeal, however, has much to do with the fact that they are perceived as incorruptible and as nonpoliticians, an excellent position to occupy in a land where the dominant political cliché is "the politician as crook." They are viewed as honest because their wealth makes it unnecessary for them to steal. Although most of them are politicians to the core, the reason that they tend to be perceived as nonpolitical is that their personal history belies the stereotype of the ward boss and the wheeler-dealer. Nixon, of course, suffered from not being one of them.

The ultimate appeal of the rich politician-celebrity, particularly the younger and more glamorous among them, is perhaps that they serve as models for millions of American mothers and fathers who would like their sons to be dedicated and good-looking, public-spirited and athletic, glamorous and honest. American parents want their children to have the advantages that Nelson Rockefeller and Edward Kennedy had. Their political appeal is based on the fact that they are what people want to be.

The discussion of the "beautiful person" in American politics flows naturally from the media's designation of Edward Kennedy as a charismatic figure. Some of the attributes of the "beautiful person" may also be those of charismatic identification. If they are, we may have pinpointed some of the sources of Kennedy's attraction in his "beautiful personality." If the attributes of the "beautiful person" are not identical to those of the charismatic leader, then we must look elsewhere to understand what is happening to Edward Kennedy's candidacy. Perhaps the best way to do this is to recapitulate the cluster of attitudes adopted toward Kennedy during the 1962 campaign, for these will show us what the media took, at that time, to be the essence of his charisma.

During the 1962 campaign, Kennedy's top aides, particularly his brother-in-law, Stephen Smith, were very concerned that the public would react adversely to Kennedy's wealth. This suggests that they did not truly understand that, in America, the rich are more loved than the poor, because they are the glory and the grandeur of the system, proof that it works, and an ideal much to be honored. The people who ran Edward Kennedy's campaign in 1962 did not understand that, in the public mind, wealth denoted political incorruptibility because the wealthy need not be concerned with the mundane and corrupting activities of business enterprise. A trade union official who advised Kennedy in 1962 on matters relating to organized labor in Massachusetts was asked whether he thought the fact that Kennedy was a millionaire would hurt him. His answer is abundantly revealing, not only of this particular issue, but of numerous strains that compose the deeper bedrock of American political culture. His comments are so rich that they bear upon the nature of prestige, aristocracy in America, the nature of work, the death of Horatio Alger, and what passes for charisma.

Some of Mr. Kennedy's staff people called me in and said, ". . . how much do you think this will hurt Mr. Kennedy — the fact that he is a millionaire, he hasn't worked very much . . ." They said, "We are deeply concerned about the fact that Mr. McCormack rose to power from one suspender and Mr. Kennedy did not." And I said, "Gentlemen, you are concerned, and I am not concerned about this at all. We find this: the working people in factories have a great respect for a man who doesn't have to climb up the ladder, for a man who has the ability or the background or the connections or the power to start from the top." And I said, "People in industrial situations have a remarkable respect for the man who doesn't have to work himself up from the dogcatcher to senator, but can start as a United States senator. They respect the power. 'Why should the man start out as a city councilman or as a clerk of the court? What good is this going to do anybody?' People today don't respect the poor little man who saved and saved and finally built up something. They respect the man who has this essential power and this essential movement." If anything, Teddy's starting from the top was to his benefit. They didn't agree with me . . .

I think the best story that is told in the campaign — that Teddy Kennedy was going through a large industrial plant. He went over to shake hands with an old machine operator; "What is it?" He said, "Teddy, I understand you never worked a day in your life." And Mr. Kennedy became concerned, and he said, "Oops, here it comes." And the fellow looked at Mr. Kennedy and said, "Let me tell you something, Teddy. You haven't missed a thing."

This is so typical of American people today. There is no honor in sweat. There is no honor in breaking your back all your life. People do respect this in Mr. Kennedy. And this I found, that they have a profound respect and reverence for him. Mr. Kennedy, with his financial holdings, could be a member of the café society international set. Mr. Kennedy could be the dean emeritus of the white trash of the café society. He could spend his winters in Cannes and his summers in Biarritz. He could be a completely non-contributing member of society with his looks, with his money, with his social connections. But instead he has chosen a life of public service. And believe me, this is what people respect.

The union official's comments, in fact, suggest that America has undergone an enormous transvaluation of values.

This description of what lies behind the Kennedy mystique is remarkable because it is clear that the basis of Edward Kennedy's strength lies in the negation of traditional American attitudes toward work and wealth, toward achievement and power, toward poverty and affluence, and in a sweeping negation of the Protestant ethic. The basis of Kennedy's alleged charisma, at least in 1962, was, metaphorically speaking, un-American. He is virtuous beyond the norm and extraordinary because he has power, because he does not have to work, because not only may he start at the top, but he has the courage to begin there. These perceived attributes are, ultimately, based upon his substantial inherited fortune. His mystique, in other words, is based on having money but not finding it necessary to labor. The secret goal of Americans may now be Kennedy's "achievement," wealth without work. The trade union official made it abundantly clear that his people saw no honor in sweat and despised the poor. The Republic was founded upon the idea that power corrupts and absolute power corrupts absolutely, and this is why the Founding Fathers created a political structure that blocks and frustrates power, that checks and balances it. But there is a new attitude toward power here, or at least an attitude toward Kennedy power, and that is that it is a precondition for doing good, for serving the public. One essential of the charismatic bond is the presumption that the charismatic leader will utilize his power for his followers. There is here no sense of the classical American attitude, that power is dangerous and potentially corrupt. A rather different argument has replaced this. The proof that powerful men will do good rather than evil lies in the fact that they reject a leisured life.

The ethic of Horatio Alger is gone. "Working people in

factories have a great respect for a man who doesn't have to climb up the ladder . . . People today don't respect the poor little man who saved and saved and finally built up something . . . There is no honor in sweat. There is no honor in breaking your back all your life." Work is no longer a virtue, thrift is no longer a virtue; in fact, it is something to be much avoided. In one of the more prophetic exchanges of the campaign, Kennedy was asked if he had ever worked a day in his life. Kennedy's response was, "Oops . . ." His alleged antagonist, but actual friend, then remarked, "Teddy, you haven't missed a thing." These are not classical American attitudes. In fact, they are antithetical to, and scornful of, that which was most venerated in nineteenth-century culture. We have here a disrespect, even hatred, for the poor, and a veneration of class and of aristocracy. For this trade union leader is really talking about the virtues of aristocracy and noblesse oblige. These unusual attitudes suggest that for a political leader to be charismatic in America, or at least to be perceived as extraordinary, his life must be a negation of American values, or, viewed differently, the fulfillment of them.

This transvaluation of values must be rooted in the material world of work. These attitudes would not be possible if people enjoyed their work, if they felt that their work was productive and useful. The alienation from labor, or the hatred of work, or the belief that those who work are exploited, lies behind the veneration of Nelson Rockefeller and Edward Kennedy. Their candidacies, in an allegedly democratic society, are possible only because the Alger ethic has been displaced by the attractions of pseudoaristocracy. Their election can be seen as a symptom of the degradation of bourgeois culture.

We have spoken of the Kennedy charisma as if it were

real, as if it were the truly viable force in the 1962 triumph. And we have noticed that the American press, before the Iranian emergency, literally could not feature an article on Kennedy without presuming that his charisma was viable and the Kennedy mystique intact. The media must have assumed, and facilely so, that charisma is transferable, and that Edward Kennedy naturally fell heir to the mantle of his brothers' majesty. But the fact is that Edward Kennedy's charisma is a creation of the press and of the Kennedys. We noted that charisma has one meaning for journalists and another for scholars. For the journalists, the charismatic candidate is one who can attract large crowds and generate and sustain excitement. He is a candidate who can evoke whistling and stomping, autographs and noise. This is loyalty and affection; it could even be the love of celebrity; but it is not charisma. If we accept Weber's definition of charisma, the classic and accepted definition among scholars, and simply ask if Kennedy fits that definition, we may discern why his popularity sharply declined during the Iranian situation. The essence of charisma, for Weber, is a perceived quality of an individual that sets him apart from ordinary men, the endowment of that person with supernatural or superhuman or exceptional powers. The power is regarded as of divine origin and the individual is treated "as a leader."

Edward Kennedy is set apart from most, but not all, ordinary men. Great wealth in America is not that rare. Edward Kennedy is set apart from ordinary men because he is the brother of a former American President. Is he endowed by his followers with supernatural and superhuman power? Is he endowed with specifically exceptional powers or qualities? The answer is no. Is he regarded as of divine origin? Obviously not. Edward Kennedy is not charismatic in the sense in which that term is used in serious scholarship. The Iranian experience, which reversed Kennedy's and Carter's standing in the polls, suggests that the famous and much publicized Kennedy charisma is a fabrication of the media and of Kennedy PR men, who repeated it so frequently that it appeared to be a self-fulfilling prophecy. If Kennedy were in fact charismatic, if the bond that united the supplicant to the Lord were truly built on faith, if Kennedy were set apart from ordinary men and endowed with extraordinary powers, the bond between him and his supporters would not have shattered in the twinkling of an Iranian eye. Kennedy Democrats not only deserted their leader, but actually preferred his enemy. This is not charisma. This is not even puppy love.

What happened between 1960, when John Fitzgerald Kennedy appeared in some charismatic guise, and 1980, when Edward Kennedy fell substantially behind the President? The Kennedy world and the real world are very different. The aura that surrounded Edward Kennedy in 1962 — the support system, as it were, that fostered what appeared to be a charismatic identification — that support system is largely gone. John Kennedy and Robert Kennedy have been assassinated; Jacqueline Kennedy is no longer an integral part of the Kennedy family; Joseph Kennedy has died; Rose Kennedy is venerable, but essentially inactive; Joan Kennedy has had serious alcohol problems; Robert Kennedy, Jr., has apparently had serious personal problems. Rumors of Edward Kennedy's womanizing are widespread, and there is, of course, Chappaquiddick. Much that is unfortunate has happened to this unusual family. It once presented a united front, a posture of power and brilliance, success and glamour, but it is now a fragmented, troubled family, and its head, Edward Kennedy, is no longer perceived as pure of heart. His image has been tarnished by Chappaquiddick, and it will continue to be so tarnished regardless of whether Edward Kennedy's report of the incident is true or false.

Charisma is a fragile attribute. The true believer's portrait of his charismatic leader is a portrait of perfection and of purity, a portrait of total power and of total goodness. The charismatic leader must either be in fact powerful and pure, or at least create the illusion that he is. But Edward Kennedy is stigmatized. The purity of his heart is in question, and the masses, who yearn for leaders who transcend the ugliness and strife of life, leaders whose appearance announces the possibility of grandeur and joy, these masses cannot tolerate the impurity. If Edward Kennedy was charismatic in 1962, that charisma has been eroded by his fringe behavior and by the disintegration of his family, which, so to speak, placed him within a framework of charismatic perception. Charisma, the attribute of his presidential brother, is not transferable, and this is the error that the media and the Kennedys have made. The mantle of charismatic identification has never been successfully transferred; neither from Jesus to Peter, nor from Caesar to his sons.

Edward Kennedy and the press assumed, fatuously, that what was, will be. The political situation in 1980 is substantially different from what it was in 1960. Edward Kennedy and his entourage can no longer count on the Kennedy mystique and the Kennedy charisma. The liberal inheritance of Franklin Roosevelt, the New Frontier of John Kennedy and the Great Society of Lyndon Johnson, is no longer the political asset it once was. Despite the alleged grandeur and glory of John Kennedy's 1000 days, the fact is that his administration accomplished very little. Despite the Johnsonian rhetoric, the significant problems that LBJ addressed remain with us in 1980. Urban blight remains a prominent feature of the American landscape. The incorporation of young blacks into the American economy has not occurred. The number of Americans on welfare and numerous other programs designed to aid the poor continues to rise, as does the cost. The war in Vietnam decimated the liberal cause and destroyed the credibility of the liberal intelligentsia. President Carter's brand of liberalism has fared no better. Liberal economists have not been able to curb inflation, and Carterian liberals have not presented a viable plan to deal with the energy shortage. Between 1960 and 1980, not only has the liberal coin been devalued, but a conservative reaction has set in, a reaction of the middle and working classes, who are fed up with the high taxes necessary to pay for welfare and dozens of other programs that they believe sustain a parasitical underclass that refuses to labor or to accept the dictates of Horatio Alger. It is because of this wellspring of conservative sentiment that Kennedy forces are concerned that their man will be tagged as a big-spending liberal. Edward Kennedy is identified with the liberal heritage, and he will suffer from its failures.

The solutions of the eighties are quite different from the solutions of the sixties. Urban problems are important, but less important. Black power is no longer the force it once was. Ethnic constituencies are not as well organized as they once were. The domestic issues of the eighties are oil, energy, OPEC, and inflation. Obviously, there are no easy solutions to these problems, since the oil-producing countries hold the upper hand. The United States, in the eighties, is moving into an era in which it no longer controls the ultimate commodity. The interjection of these issues, coupled with a decline of American power, has unsettled the electorate and altered the traditional cleavage between so-called liberals and conservatives. Edward Kennedy, long identified with classical New Deal liberalism, must re-establish an identity on complex and difficult terrain.

The situation in foreign policy is not dissimilar. The Cold War issues and the Vietnam War, with which John Kennedy and Lyndon Johnson were preoccupied, have been replaced by a desperate concern for oil and other sources of energy. These problems are also less amenable to the will of the State Department. The facile solutions to issues of foreign policy that John Kennedy propounded will meet with even less success at the hands of his successors. The issues in 1980 may be more intractable — hostages in Iran and invasions of Afghanistan — but the powers of incumbency are obvious. The ayatollah made Carter. Regardless of what Edward Kennedy may do during the remainder of the 1980 campaign, foreign policy is the preserve of the President of the United States, no matter how unsuccessful that policy is. With the approach of the Iowa primary, there was no Democratic presidential campaign in this country. Kennedy has even been robbed of the possibility of confronting Carter. Such are the vagaries of presidential elections. If the charisma of Edward Kennedy were in full flower, if he were perceived as extraordinary and unique, he would have maintained his support even through the Iranian situation. The fact that he did not is witness to his ordinary mortality.

The election of 1980 is among the more unusual in our history, for its outcome will be largely the result of foreign intrigue. The ayatollah and the Kremlin may have played a more decisive role than Jimmy Carter and Edward Kennedy.

8

Election 1980

PRESIDENTIAL ELECTIONS have been studied extensively by political scientists and commercial pollsters since the thirties. Hundreds of books have been written on the voting behavior of the American electorate. Thousands of polls have been taken, ranging from national samples of the entire electorate to cross sections of different socioeconomic classes, races, ideological groupings, professions, religious groups, and members of "deviant" parties. The data are voluminous, and many sophisticated theories have been constructed to account for how and why Americans vote as they do. These data have practical significance for campaign managers. Pollsters can determine what various groups are concerned with. They can identify potential supporters who are inactive. They can sometimes locate support that is evaporating. They can even suggest what strategies are likely to be rational.

American voters are significantly less active than voters in European democracies. Approximately one-half of the electorate customarily fails to vote in presidential elections, and voting turnout is substantially lower in congressional and state elections. More than one-third of the electorate never participates in politics and another third votes only in presidential elections. The proportion of Americans who work for candidates, contribute money, and pay serious attention to the campaign rarely exceeds one in ten.

Political apathy is the result of a widespread belief that it makes little or no difference who wins elections. This belief reflects the fact that the overwhelming majority of Americans agree on fundamental political and economic values. The American people, and both political parties, believe deeply in the virtues of representative government and of capitalism, and neither seriously considers any alternative. Politics, which historically has dealt with the issue of how a society should best organize its economy and polity, is therefore "superfluous" in America because these issues were resolved in the late eighteenth century. The apathy of the great majority is certainly a result of consensus as well as contentment. For blacks and other outsiders, apathy is often a result of powerlessness and alienation.

The basic fact of American electoral politics is the long-term plurality of Democrats. Since the Great Depression, the Republicans have never recouped their strength, and in 1976, 39 percent of Americans identified themselves as Democrats. The Republican party enters the 1980 election with the support of only 23 percent of the eligible electorate. Party identification is a critical variable, because the overwhelming majority of Americans vote for the candidate of "their" party. Americans shift their vote occasionally, but they rarely change their party, and when they do, it is usually in response to a major Depression or a charismatic candidate. Americans tend to vote consistently for the same party, and this gives the Democrats a substantial advantage.

The critical shift in American party politics since the fifties has been the dramatic increase in the number who identify themselves as independents. Since 1950 the proportion of independents has risen from 20 to 36 percent. Independents now outnumber Republicans. The GOP is now a "third" party, and the Democrats could easily become the opposition party if the trend toward independence continues. No candidate for the presidency can now win without the support of a substantial block of independents. Campaign managers wish to know who independents are and what they respond to, since they now constitute the largest bloc of "free-floating" voters. They shift from party to party with much greater frequency than do partisans, so much so that since 1940, both the Republican and Democratic party have captured the independent vote. The stereotype of the independent as apolitical and disinterested in politics is false. Independents rank just a bit below Democrats and Republicans in terms of voting frequency and political sophistication; they are, however, more likely than the party-affiliated to vote in terms of candidates and personalities rather than party or ideology. This could be an important factor in the 1980 election. The Republican candidates are committed to a fairly rigid conservative stance, and none is perceived as charismatic or a celebrity. But Edward Kennedy does appear to some as the heir to Camelot, the brother of slain martyrs, and American ego-ideal who can run more as a Kennedy than a Democrat.

Both parties need the support of independents, but the Republicans, preferred by a little less than one-fourth of the electorate, need the overwhelming majority of independents to win. The strategies of both parties are affected by this fact. Democratic candidates can enjoy the luxury of courting traditional constituences, the groups with whom they feel ideologically simpatico. They can maintain their ideological coherence. They can also seek independent support by moving slightly to the center, or what amounts to the right, without fear of losing their traditional liberal constituency. Since there are no parties to the left of the Democrats, liberals who might be dissatisfied with a centrist turn by Kennedy or Carter simply have no place to turn. Their liberal options are closed because Reagan and Bush are substantially more conservative than Carter or Kennedy.

The Democrats have more flexibility on issues; the Republicans are caught in a bind. They must maintain solid support among Republicans. To do this, they must serve traditional conservative fare. To win millions of independent votes, however, they must temper their conservatism with liberal appeals. In either case, they seek one constituency at the expense of the other. This is why Republicans might be wise to play down the Republican label, campaign as qualified individuals, and advance "classless" and "apolitical" solutions.

Four decades of research into the political behavior of the American voter have uncovered many other facts and theories that bear on the 1980 election. Edward Kennedy, for example, need not be concerned that his Catholicism is a significant disadvantage. We know that Catholics identify more strongly with the Democratic party than Protestants, although Protestants in America greatly outnumber Catholics. Religion, long a central issue in American elections (witness the defeat of Al Smith), became much less significant with John Kennedy's election. Public-opinion polls in the 1970s indicate that relatively few Americans would vote for or against a candidate solely on religious grounds.

Low-income groups, a significant Democratic constituency, vote less frequently than the more affluent. The highest rate of nonvoters is among blacks, who were also the most staunch supporters of JFK, Johnson, and Carter. Republicans are comforted by the fact that this Democratic stronghold is apathetic, and this is why Democrats spend a substantial portion of their assets in black ghettos and impoverished urban areas. Their goal is to stimulate interest and increase turnout. Democrats since FDR remind poor blacks and whites that it was they who initiated Social Security, unemployment compensation, collective bargaining, welfare, food stamps, Medicare, and job retraining, and that most of the programs were passed in the face of Republican opposition. This strategy has succeeded, and the effort to increase turnout among the urban poor in 1980 should also succeed because the energy shortage and inflation will stimulate interest, raise voter participation, and help Democrats.

If Kennedy wins the nomination, he will make a substantial effort to reach apathetic voters. Extensive efforts will be concentrated in black, Chicano, and Puerto Rican ghettos and the poorest sections of metropolitan areas. The Kennedy campaign will establish special task forces assigned to those areas to remind blacks and the poor how and why they would benefit by voting, and by voting for Kennedy. The leadership of these task forces will have an ethnic and racial composition that matches the target constituency. This effort will be a major undertaking. The media will be blanketed with the message that Kennedy fought relentlessly for programs beneficial to the underprivileged. The struggle for national health insurance will be featured. Video tapes will be made that show Kennedy arguing that cities should not lose tax revenues, because the victims will be "the elderly poor, the blacks, and the inner city youth." The message, originally designed for Harlem and Watts, will be a variation of an old Kennedy theme:

"While economic growth is important for all Americans, it is absolutely essential for black Americans. It is the indispensable condition of black progress."

If past Kennedy campaigns are indicative, and if Kennedy does not falter at the convention, the apparatus to get this message across will be specifically designed for the inactive poor. Millions of brochures and handouts will be printed, and thousands of storefronts will be rented as headquarters. Block-by-block campaign organizations will be set up, and time will be purchased on ethnic and black radio stations to convey the message that Kennedy has supported, and will support, the creation of more jobs and better housing for the poor, increased welfare and Social Security benefits, tax cuts, occupational training centers for unemployed youth, public day care centers, drug rehabilitation programs, national health insurance, integrated schools, and rigid enforcement of equal opportunity laws.

These programs leave Kennedy open to several charges. He has been tagged as a "big-spending liberal," a candidate who wants to allocate billions for social welfare and health, money primarily destined for low-income groups.

He also has been attacked for fanning inflation and raising taxes, but this will not be the critical thrust. He will be perceived as the candidate who not only increases the burdens of the middle class, but increases these burdens for a dubious purpose — to aid and comfort the lazy and parasitical poor.

President Carter, as early as October 1979, launched the attack. "Senator Kennedy is much more inclined toward the old philosophy of pouring out new programs and new money to meet a social need. I disagree with him." *Time* writers see the charge as perhaps Kennedy's "biggest liability." "Kennedy," they argue, "advocates substantial spending and more liberalism at a time when many public-opinion analysts believe Americans have become more conservative."

Kennedy may be more vulnerable than even his critics believe, for his liberalism runs counter to a political posture that has been growing for twenty years, a posture we call "conservative populism." Conservative populism is a more strident and racist version of traditional American conservatism. It is a reaction to the tax burdens placed on the middle class and on working people, in part, to support the welfare of blacks and the poor. The corrosive effects of inflation have exacerbated this conservatism, as have busing, feminism, the demand for homosexual rights, the abortion issue, and the perceived decline of American morals.

Conservative populism is a fusion of laissez faire and libertarianism, a demand for deregulation of the economy and sharp curtailment of social welfare, coupled with a defense of the moral right of American working people *not* to pay for welfare or food stamps or ADC, the right *not* to bus their children, the right to prohibit abortions, the right to prohibit homosexuals from teaching in public schools, and so forth. Conservative populism is not merely opposition to public spending or the obligation to care for the poor, it is a posture of extreme self-interest, a world view that is the negation of social responsibility. It is conservative in its defense of the absolute rights of property and laissez faire, and populist in its defense of the right of working people to exercise their popular sovereignty to retain more and give away less. It is a retreat to privatism and self-interest in the name of liberty.

Conservative populism contains an explicit theory of class struggle and an implicit theory of racism. The theory of class struggle is the reverse of Marx's doctrine that the rich exploit the poor. The new conservatives believe that the productive classes, the classes who labor, produce useful products, and obey the precepts of Horatio Alger are being robbed of the rightful fruits of their labor by the government in behalf of parasites and unproductive idlers — welfare recipients who could work but choose not to; millions who are sustained by unemployment compensation, able to work, but not willing; and an endless parade of stragglers, all on the public dole and all recipients of the largesse of the working and middle classes. This transfer of working people's money to a shiftless underclass is seen as a gigantic revival of Robin Hood — the sweat of working people is transformed into milk and honey for the poor.

The anger of the working class is compounded by the fact that many of the poor are black, Puerto Rican, and Chicano. The lower middle class, long the most intolerant in America, is fearful of falling into the ranks of the dispossessed. Their status is fragile, supported only by those below them. A runaway inflation could easily decimate their security and denude them of status.

No one knows how deep this current is. But Edward Kennedy will not be its beneficiary. As the campaign progresses, Kennedy's opponents will make it clear that he has one of the most liberal records in the Senate and that he has supported almost every program that benefits the poor and the unemployed and minority groups. If Reagan and Bush are clear-headed in this matter, they will make the latent feelings of the lower middle class explicit and very public. The costs of welfare and other programs for the poor should be publicized by Republicans, along with a breakdown of increased tax burdens. The connection between rising taxes and rising social welfare costs should be made obvious. An even more grandiose perspective is available to Republicans. They should argue that the very foundations of American civilization are threatened by an underclass eating away at the healthy core of capitalism, eroding our moral posture, destroying the Protestant ethic, and debasing the wages of labor. The issue is obviously far more complex and explosive than the mere spending of money.

The problem is critical for the Democrats because the constituency that traditionally supports the party of FDR, the lower middle class, is now attracted to conservative populism. Robin Hood is no longer a heroic figure in America and Horatio Alger is not respected.

If Kennedy is the nominee, a counterstrategy is available. The Democratic candidate is the liberal candidate. There is neither party nor candidate of significance to his left. Having nothing to fear from an attack on the left, but some concern with a populist attack from the right, Kennedy should move to the center, mute his liberal label, and yet, when necessary, cater to big labor and the urban poor. Kennedy began to employ this strategy in 1979. Although he supported liberal legislation for years, he is now trying to avoid the liberal label. During the seventies, the designation *liberal* became an epithet. For millions, it now means massive federal spending for impractical and dubious purposes that results in increased taxes for the working class and millions living off the public dole. Kennedy now presents himself as a pragmatist. PR men are characterizing him as a hardheaded problem solver, unencumbered by ideology. During the year 1979, he accommodated himself to many constituencies. When he defines the "legitimate" demands of the American people to include a vast array of public services, he sounds like a socialist. At other times, he echoes the thoughts of Adam Smith and staunchly supports classical nineteenth-century laissez faire. "We are making a clean break with the New Deal, and even the 1960s," he said in New York. "We reject the idea that government knows best across the board, that public planning is inherently superior or more effective than private action . . . government intervention in the economy should come only as a last resort." Reagan, of course, agrees.

Edward Kennedy, like his brothers, is flexible. (Some critics say the Kennedys are without principle.) He has advocated the deregulation of the trucking industry and airlines, and simultaneously he has favored substantial restrictions on corporate mergers and vigorous enforcement of antitrust laws. He is also quite capable of mystifying issues, shifting his position on them, and ignoring them. For example, he urged a $4-billion cut in the defense budget and then voted for a substantial increase. Originally, he argued for a national health insurance plan that would replace all private programs. Now he favors a plan in which employers extend the benefits they already provide.

Kennedy is a highly skilled professional politician in the best American tradition. He trades, deals, compromises, backtracks, and has both a public and private face. He is eminently pragmatic and will meet the challenge of conservative populism if forced to. As Reagan, Connally, or Bush is forced to become less conservative in search of independent votes and Kennedy assumes an even more centrist position, the candidates will come to resemble each other more as the campaign progresses. The traditional pattern of American politics and presidential elections will then reassert itself as the American consensus on free enterprise frames the question.

In addition to combating conservative populism, Kennedy should pursue other strategic gambits. He must advance traditional liberal bread-and-butter programs to reinforce the Democratic majority, particularly the black constituency and the urban poor. He should make the campaign as exciting as possible by maximizing the alleged Kennedy charisma, securing the services of Jackie Onassis for an occasional performance and parading Rose Kennedy before urban Catholics. If Kennedy defeats Carter for the nomination, the campaign should also memorialize John Kennedy. If interest is high, Democrats are more likely to vote.

This is the strategy. Coopt the center, deny Republicans a constituency, but maintain the liberal prerogative. Capitalize on, and celebrate, the Camelot legend and the Kennedy mystique. Cater to the urban poor and deftly imply that Edward Kennedy's election might symbolize, not only resurrection and renewal but also an opportunity for transcendence of the guilt incurred at John Kennedy's death.

*

We have spoken of the issues Kennedy might pursue, but we have not discussed the significance of issues to the American voter. Civics teachers are fond of telling students that Americans are vitally interested in issues. These teachers may be patriotic, but they are naive. Only one in five Americans is politically sophisticated. This 20 percent use terms such as "liberal" and "conservative" and clearly understand their meaning. They know how the candidates stand on some issues, and many have ideas about where the country should go and how it should get there.

A substantially larger group, about one in three, are exclusively concerned with which party will best advance the interest of their immediate group. These voters tend to conceive of American politics in terms of two classic clichés:

"Democrats are good for the working man," and "Republicans are for big business." These may be slogans, but they are not without merit. In general, working people actually do do better when Democrats are in power, and trade unions do benefit greatly from legislation sponsored by Democrats. Business is less restricted under Republican administrations, and corporate executives do play a greater role in Republican administrations. A voter who relates the self-interest of his group to a political party is by no means unsophisticated.

One-fourth of the electorate operate on the relatively primitive assumption that the "nature of the times" is better or worse when a particular party is in power. Without specifying any policies that parties might follow, voters concerned with the nature of the times frequently comment that the times require a Republican or a Democrat.

But there are millions of voters who do not think of politics in terms of "the times" or of anything else. Approximately one-fifth of the electorate are "know-nothings," people with literally no knowledge of politics. When asked why they are Democrats, they reply, "I have always been a Democrat." Their most common responses to pollsters are "I vote for the man," "It's time for a change," and "I don't know." They have little or no interest in politics.

These data reconfirm the soundness of the Kennedy strategies we suggested earlier. One critical gambit relates to the "know-nothings." Since they react almost exclusively to the personal attributes of candidates and to sloganizing, Kennedy should play upon his alleged charisma and the motif of John Kennedy's death. The appeal of these symbols, however, is obviously not restricted to the politically illiterate.

But there is a wider issue here. Given the lack of political sophistication of Americans and the minimal interest in issues, how should a presidential candidate present his views? On what level should he introduce and evaluate policy alternatives and explain the variety of benefits likely to follow? One answer might be, on a level that could be understood by someone in the sixth or eighth grade.

Such is not the case. In the first place, the traditions of the nation require that candidates for the presidency of the United States make a dignified and serious presentation of the issues. The national facade, the public face, demands serious consideration for what is advertised as our most solemn exercise of popular sovereignty. Candidates apparently feel this pressure or assume that a serious stance is persuasive. There are, however, sound political reasons for taking a sophisticated approach to campaign issues, preferably a highly sophisticated approach. The Kennedys understood this when Teddy Kennedy first ran for the Senate. A candidate who presents issues with sophisticated elaboration — charts, tables, data, proofs, comparisons, lots of facts and historical references — and relates these to the future well-being of his constituency appears to be knowledgeable and on top of things, even if he is not really understood. The Kennedys understood that a barrage of statistics and a driving presentation are far more impressive than the data themselves. They realized that sophisticated rhetoric has an important latent political function. Words and figures are taken not for their intrinsic meaning, but for their symbolic effect.

We have presented the fundamental characteristics of the American voter and suggested some campaign strategies for Kennedy and his opponents. The voter is his ultimate target, but his immediate goal is delegate support and the nomination.

*

National nominating conventions are unique political events. They resemble neither elections nor legislative struggles. At times conventions have been controlled by a handful of power brokers, cabals, or backstage conspiracies. Revolts from the floor have occurred occasionally, though democratic uprisings have been rare. This is because, traditionally, conventions have been the preserve of professional politicians, senators, governors, city bosses, all power brokers with strong personal loyalties and years of practice in the art of quid pro quo. These factions want to nominate a winner, but they also want a deal for themselves and their circle.

Until the mid-sixties, a hierarchy of power and control existed in almost every state delegation. Professional politicians, often mayors of large cities or the bosses of machines, were able to dispense enough goodies among their rank and file to control many votes. Their stock of patronage at any given time was often large enough to ensure the delivery of some delegates, and their future promissory notes were credible enough to entice the recalcitrant.

Convention politics traditionally revolved around the candidates' attempt to convert power brokers — perhaps as many as 200 of them. Candidates did not abandon the chase for individual delegates; they courted individual delegates avidly. This was particularly true of candidates who were neither incumbents nor favorites and were thus deprived of patronage. Large numbers of delegates were also professionals, lesser office holders, or regular party workers. Each state had its separate party organization, which was more disciplined than the national organization. Delegates, therefore, were often beholden to state and city party leaders. It was the custom for a handful of state leaders to hold the status of "favorite son." By so doing, they were able to command the loyalty of their state delegation, at least until the first ballot was completed. This tactic increased the bargaining power of the favorite son and the state delegation. In exchange for their support on a critical ballot, the state party organization extracted the promise of patronage and federal largesse from the nominee if he were elected.

The relation between nominee and state party boss was essentially the same as that between boss and delegates — that is, it was based on the exchange of patronage for votes. The state party leader controlled his delegation by the promise of future patronage or the continuation of an existing political job. In this process, power brokers were forced to make two critical estimates. They had to estimate who among the nominees was most likely to be elected, and they had to throw their support to them when it was still much in demand. If the party nominated a candidate who lost, the greatest source of federal patronage was closed for at least four years. Jobs, programs, and money were the coinage of conventions.

A striking example of this occurred in 1979 and involved the heir to the great Daley machine in Chicago. The current mayor, Jane Byrne, was wooed assiduously by Jimmy Carter precisely because she does head the last great city machine. She endorsed Kennedy at a time when he was "weak," and if he wins, she can expect a handsome reward for the city and her own political future.

The example of Jane Byrne is noteworthy because it is now so rare. The great urban political machines have been decimated. Their function as social service agencies for the poor has been taken over by the federal government, and their ethnic constituencies no longer need so much political succor.

After the 1968 Democratic convention in Chicago, which was plagued by anti-Vietnam riots and disruption, the party drastically revised the rules by which delegates are selected and conventions are governed. The crucial change that resulted from these reforms was the virtual removal of control over the selection of delegates by party functionaries. Senators, governors, and mayors were denied control of the selection of loyal delegates bound by ties of patronage and party loyalty.

The essence of the reform was to increase greatly the number of primary elections at which delegates are selected. Three-fourths of the delegates are now selected at primary elections. Even states that select delegates by caucus, like Iowa, have opened their caucuses to all comers. The result has been a tremendous increase in grassroots politicking among amateur activists. The proportion of amateur delegates has risen drastically since 1968 and has become greater with each convention.

The impact of this reform was so great that two-thirds of the delegates to the 1976 Democratic convention had never been to a convention before. The amateurs, regardless of race or sex, tend to be well educated, seriously concerned with issues, and strongly committed to the candidate for whom they have publicly declared. Unlike the professionals whom they have displaced, these amateurs are concerned less with the electability of candidates than they are with the issues they advocate. This bias is the true sign of an amateur.

Selection of delegates by primary election is not the only device that has greatly weakened the dominance of power brokers. Because of two developments, state delegations are no longer unified blocs. Party rules specify that a candidate who receives at least 15 percent of the primary vote receives a proportionate share of the delegates from his or her state. State delegations now tend to be factionalized, and this makes it difficult or impossible for professionals or any one candidate to control large numbers. In the actual balloting, these factions do have a voice because the "unit rule" has been abolished. That rule required state delegations to vote as a bloc for the candidate with a plurality of the delegates. The candidates now receive votes according to the pledges of delegates. The convention has not only been factionalized and turned over to amateurs, it has been radically democratized.

These changes have drastically altered the politics of nominating conventions. Party professionals knew this would happen. Before the 1976 Democratic primaries, many of the old pros predicted that the convention would be deadlocked. They understood that amateurs, unlike themselves, were less likely to compromise, because they were so committed to candidates and ideologies. Electability was no longer the sole criterion. For professionals, this change was tantamount to a suicide attempt. The likelihood of a deadlock was increased by the abolition of the "winner take all" rule. Now, blocs of minorities, selected in primaries, could create a situation in which no single candidate would go to the convention with enough votes to win.

The new system enormously increases the importance of primaries, campaign organization, and financial support. Candidates must now attempt to win enough primaries to capture the nomination on the first ballot, as Carter did in 1976. If this does not occur, a deadlock is quite possible.

The new primary and convention rules make Kennedy's problem more difficult, yet they also ease his burden. The rules substantially reduce an incumbent President's ability to dictate the nominee, be it himself or his successor. The traditional attitude toward a sitting President who sought renomination was fear and respect. To challenge the incumbent meant political suicide because the President was likely to win and, therefore, could retaliate by cutting off patronage. Presidential control of patronage is still important. Almost every important political leader in New York State, many of whom had supported John and Robert Kennedy, publicly endorsed Carter in 1979. (Two of the most powerful, Senator Moynihan and Governor Carey, remained silent.) The unspoken reason why ex-Kennedy men now support Carter was clear to all. The President controls the dispensation of great political plums for New York City and other cities, such as Buffalo and Rochester, as well as for New York State, and he will control patronage at least through January 1981. When New York City Mayor Koch and his colleagues declared, many newspapers took this as a sign of Kennedy's weakness. This is not necessarily the case. They had little choice, and if Kennedy does well in the spring primaries and looks like a winner, Senator Moynihan and the governor, and Koch and colleagues, will make new friends, perhaps in June or July.

But the new rules have created an influx of amateurs, outside the control of senators, governors, and mayors. The professionals can still influence some delegates, but it is now a small minority of the total. Their endorsement is helpful, but not critical. They can mobilize whatever remains of their personal entourages and their campaign organizations for the President. But there is little else they can do. The President cannot dictate the nomination because the professionals whom he may influence have, in turn, little power to deliver delegates. This obviously helps Kennedy and makes an assault on the incumbent more feasible. Kennedy may also benefit from the army of amateurs because his staunch liberalism would appeal to their stress on ideology.

The new rules also increase the chance that more candidates can survive the first ballot, and this could have an effect on convention strategy. Prior to the rule changes, if a candidate were clearly unable to win the nomination, his delegates were likely to switch on the second or third ballot to another candidate. In 1960 John Kennedy feared that he could not discipline his troops through a couple of ballots because electability was far more important to delegates than ideology or personality. Now, however, amateurs deeply committed to a particular candidate are willing to hold out for several ballots. The vote now tends to be less volatile and recalcitrant, and uncommitted delegates have potentially far greater influence. The situation becomes both more and less stable.

The perception of Kennedy as a winner, at least before the events in Iran, and even possibly after them, should help him with party professionals. Senators and congressmen in need of Kennedy's coattails — and there are many — should be responsive. Indeed, for several months before Kennedy announced, a large bloc of congressmen, primarily from New England, the Middle Atlantic states, and the industrial centers of the Midwest, urged him to run because their constituencies were in serious economic trouble. These states have hundreds of delegates and millions of voters, and most of their congressmen have decided that Carter's economic policies have failed, that Carter is not electable, and that Kennedy will reintroduce Keynesian incentives to the economy. The support of so many members of the House can only help.

A similar dynamic operates in the Senate. Senate Democrats now have a majority of fifty-eight to forty-one, with one independent. Twenty-four Democrats stand for re-election in 1980, and eleven will be involved in close contests. They may need the aid of a popular presidential candidate: In 1978, with Carter as President, almost one-half of the incumbent Democrats involved in closely contested elections were beaten.

In evaluating the substantial increase in popularity that the ayatollah has bestowed upon Carter, readers should bear in mind that Carter's weakness in the Senate can hardly be exaggerated. It is highly unusual for an incumbent President to have such meager support among senators of his own party.

If Kennedy can enter the convention with enough delegates to leave the issue in doubt, he may benefit more than Carter from the influx of amateurs. During four years in the White House, Carter has become known as an inept professional who bears the stigma of inflation and the energy crises. Kennedy, however, has the reputation of a liberal ideologue, a vigorous advocate of national health insurance and criminal-justice reform, and an opponent of corporate mergers. Furthermore, he is not held responsible for current crises. This image could appeal. Although Kennedy has become a consummate professional politician during his years in the Senate, his reputation, strangely enough, is not that of a wheeler-dealer, but rather that of a fighter for good causes.

The Kennedys have demonstrated their expertise in convention politics. In 1960, with limited access to power brokers, John Kennedy's search for delegates was highly refined and meticulous. His managers maintained extensive files on delegates, indexed and cross-indexed, with extensive information on age, race, sex, occupation, hobbies, friends, political contacts, and political aspirations. Attention to details of this kind permitted John Kennedy to husband his time efficiently, concentrate on "possibles," and avoid those definitely committed for or against him.

For the staff and the candidate, the delegate hunt is an arduous undertaking, exhausting for the candidate, time-consuming, expensive, and often inefficient. Thousands of delegates must be contacted, and the time is limited. Staff people must maintain an accurate running tally of delegates firmly committed to the opposition so that time need not be wasted in wooing them. Estimates must be made of those who play a coquettish waiting game, those who may be seduced, and those who may not. The task that can really pay off is the compilation of a meticulous dossier of delegate desires, most of which are really quite petty. Some delegates may want a photograph of the candidate for use in a future race for the city council. A delegate who seeks an appointment to West Point for her daughter may see the candidate as the key to her heart's desire. Another is willing to go either way in exchange for a promise to grant entry to the United States for a relative from Russia. In the main, these are small requests. Delegates who are ideologues demand more — a pledge to curtail the construction of nuclear plants, a commitment to conservation, or a national health insurance plan. The request may be large or small, personal or ideological, but the question is which candidate is aware of them and who gets there first.

At the start of the campaign, before the ayatollah became Carter's major asset, the question of who would win the Democratic nomination appeared to be settled. One had only to contrast Kennedy's success as a liberal in the Senate with Carter's dismal record on inflation and energy, or Carter's blandness with the Kennedy mystique. Or one could compare Kennedy's vigor with the President's passivity. Or ask, before the Iranian crisis, who has the longest coattails, Carter or Kennedy. Or who is the heir to Camelot, or who bears the Kennedy mystique.

The answer obviously is Kennedy, but Jimmy Carter is the President of the United States, and he is the leader of the Democratic party. The President's resources and patronage are extensive. His roots in the party are deep. He has been dispensing hundreds of millions of dollars throughout the country, numerous federal offices and massive programs, for three years, and is now ready to call in his bets. Although few political writers gave the President a serious chance of defeating Kennedy in the fall of 1979, most assumed that Carter, at the very least, had enough support to so embitter and divide the convention that Kennedy's chances in November would be sharply curtailed.

This scenario, widely shared by political columnists throughout the country before the Iran and Afghanistan emergencies and before the very adverse publicity about Chappaquiddick, was based on the common assumption that the Kennedy charisma was operative and the most compelling force in presidential politics, a presence that transcended earthly political realities. When the subject of a political strategy for Carter arose, even the most sophisticated Washington correspondents were assured that Carter's main task was to demystify Kennedy. David Broder of the *Washington Post*, Hedrick Smith of the *New York Times*, and Mary McGrory, for example, asserted that if demystification were to be achieved, Carter would have to deal with Kennedy's alleged womanizing and Chappaquiddick. They thought an attack along these lines would be difficult, and if not done with taste, could easily backfire because millions who perceived Kennedy as charismatic would be outraged. Regardless of what so-called political experts write after events in Iran and Iowa, the reader is well advised to remember that literally no one thought Carter would win, and that very few thought either that the Kennedy charisma was fragile or that it was a creation of the media and of the Kennedys, rather than a real force in and of itself. This is, in part, because most analysts do not understand what a charismatic bond is.

This leads us to an analysis of political strategies of our own design and of strategies suggested by some of the most professional and astute campaign managers in the country, all proposed before the Iranian emergency. (Several professionals suggested that Carter not even contest the nomination.) In retrospect, most of the plans have an archaic and naive quality, although it was occasionally suggested that Carter's only hope was an international crisis.

*

The nomination of a President of the United States for a second term is customarily taken for granted. Presidents have been challenged, on rare occasion, when a major wing of the party believes that a compelling moral issue can be resolved only by running a new candidate, regardless of the consequences. The Vietnam War is a case in point. Teddy Roosevelt's splitting the Republican party is another. Compromise is impossible if key issues are framed in stark moral terms, in terms of good and evil, in terms of how life should be lived. But Edward Kennedy's challenge is not framed in moral dichotomies, and this is one reason why he finds it difficult to justify his contention. It is also a reason why the polls indicate that many Americans perceive his candidacy as intrusive and "illegitimate."

The President may also be opposed when party leaders and a very large segment of delegates are convinced that he will lose. Before the attack on our embassy in Iran, the polls indicated not only that Carter was behind Kennedy by nearly two to one, but that he was also running behind Bush and Reagan. Many Democratic politicians were convinced in the fall of 1979 that Carter would lose. Kennedy would not have run unless he was also convinced of this. When the factors that shaped the outcome of the election become clear, it may be seen to be the case that when Carter prospered because of the hostages, and overwhelmed Kennedy in the polls and in Iowa, Kennedy's candidacy was robbed of its legitimacy because Carter looked like a winner and Kennedy had no moral cause.

The Carter candidacy is weak on several counts. Presidents, rightly or wrongly, are held responsible for the nation's troubles, and Carter is no doubt another presidential victim. The energy crisis persists and he has failed to develop a feasible program for supplying additional energy or alternative forms. Prices continue to rise, and unemployment is high (though not rising). We now have double-digit inflation, and the American Dream of affluence and ease is in danger of eroding. The American people customarily respond to economic trouble by blaming incumbents and voting for their opponents. Herbert Hoover's replacement by Franklin Roosevelt is a classic example of what economic collapse can do to the party in power.

Carter, we noted, is clearly the victim of holding presidential office during hard times. Although he has been effective in forging a bipartisan foreign policy on issues such as SALT, the Middle East, and the Panama Canal, it is his misfortune that these issues are not the kind that are easily convertible into votes. The constraints imposed by OPEC probably negate the possibility of a successful domestic energy program — Kennedy's program as well as Carter's — but the President is hard put to explain this to the American people. The advantage for a challenger is that he can criticize the program of the White House without the need to prove the feasibility of his own scheme.

But facts often do not determine the outcome of conventions and elections. Mr. Carter's problem is that the President has become the personification of the federal government, good or bad, and the person from whom people expect action and solutions, not failures. He suffers because of inflation and prospers because of the Iranian situation. Richard Neustadt, author of a leading work on the presidency, has noted Carter's dilemma: "Especially in troubled times, the public wants the President to deal with issues like inflation and the economy that are essentially beyond his control." During 1979 the Gallup Poll showed a statistical correlation between the President's declining "approval rating" and the rising rate of inflation. Millions conceive of the President as actually running the country, obviously an illusion, but for the President a sad fact of incumbency. The tendency to exaggerate the real powers of the President, to make the office larger than life, explains, in part, why Kennedy selected "leadership" as *the* issue. The illusion of omnicompetent Presidential power and the contrasting reality work greatly to the advantage of the challenger. How can a President make the case for his ability as a leader when the country is caught in spiraling inflation?

But Carter is vulnerable not only because he is the incumbent. In 1976 he had the advantage of being an obscure former governor of Georgia, running against an ineffectual President and the Washington establishment. He now symbolizes Washington, and he is the leader of that establishment, which is perceived by millions as a failure in domestic affairs. He cannot run on the slogan, "Throw the rascals out." He cannot run against Gerald Ford. In fact, he must run against himself. He no longer has the benefit of the Watergate legacy, a legacy that permitted him to appeal to the nation's desire for honor and decency. In fact, his reputation may now be tarnished. He has been investigated by a federal agency. His intimate friend, Bert Lance, is currently under investigation, and he is the brother of Billy Carter.

In 1980 he cannot run on the issue of morality in public office, as he did in 1976, because the prime issue is the effectiveness, not the morality, of his administration. His ultimate weakness, and one not easily overcome, is his image as a weak and ineffective leader. Literally every public-opinion poll indicates that large numbers of people find Carter to be indecisive. Circumstances in Iran may have been the turning point of the campaign for many reasons, but the critical effect of the situation was undoubtedly to re-create Carter in a Churchillian mold, the President at war, bold, resourceful, and tough. The situation in Teheran has apparently obscured the old and ineffective Mr. Carter.

Before the problems in Iran and Afghanistan, political consultants suggested that Carter's first task was to use the presidential office to counteract his image as a weak and ineffectual leader. Although the Iranian crisis reversed his image, Carter's aides advised the President to solidify his new-found strength by continuing to use the office in a vigorous way. The Iranian affair may turn out to be a double quirk of fate. It not only counteracted Carter's appearance of weakness, but also robbed Kennedy of his key issue, leadership.

*

The powers of the presidency are vast and they can be used for immediate and practical political advantage as well as high state policy. The fact that Carter came to this realization so late in his term is an indication of his political naiveté. The President has frequently not followed the first rule of practical politics: Reward your friends and punish your enemies. One political consultant who has worked with liberal Democrats commented on the proper use of patronage during a campaign. "If you're running for mayor, and you have limited resources, and it is September and October, you fix the streets in the wards where you need votes."

In autumn of 1979, Carter began to dispense patronage precisely where he needs votes. In October he made a series of trips around the country, leaving what he calls the "island" of Washington, trips designed to make contact with the grassroots, particularly Catholics and labor. He blamed Congress more frequently and attacked special interests and the oil lobby. He reiterated the theme that the President single-handedly cannot cure all the nation's problems, and he argued, probably with reason, that when Kennedy presented his agenda, it would seem pale compared to his own.

During the fall of 1979, he began to use the presidential office primarily for political purposes. His appointments were made to rebuild ethnic constituencies. Moon Landrieu, a liberal Catholic mayor of New Orleans, was appointed to the cabinet, as was Neil Goldschmidt, a westerner and a Jew. Benjamin Civiletti, a Catholic Italian-American, was appointed attorney general. Carter plans to appoint an Hispanic-American to head the new Department of Education. The business community got what it wanted, a true conservative, Paul Volcker, to chair the Federal Reserve Board. Feminists were, no doubt, pleased when the President elevated a second woman to a senior post in the White House. The President was obviously concerned by Kennedy's candidacy and had decided to use his office to reward friends and punish enemies.

Three months before the Iowa caucuses, he ordered the government to lend $13 million to a cooperative in Humboldt, Iowa. Four months before the New Hampshire primary, he designated economic aid for Berlin, New Hampshire. Prior to receiving the endorsement of several prominent politicians in New York State, the President allocated substantial funds for hospitals in New York City and other projects in the state. Professional politicians, mayors, governors, and congressmen know that regardless of who is elected, Carter will control billions of dollars until January 1981, monies that could be allocated to their districts. This beneficence could materially aid their reelection. Many will probably desert Carter if they conclude that Kennedy has the nomination, but until then, political wisdom dictates their allegiance to the White House.

The more aggressively Carter disperses his blessings, the greater are his chances in the primaries. This is vintage Kennedy politics and Carter is fast becoming a master practitioner. Florida is a case in point. Just before the straw vote, which he won, Carter dispensed almost $20 million for public housing in Dade County, and $5 million for the Orlando airport. The President could strengthen his support by dispensing many more favors. He could set up a telephone barrage to delegates from states that hold early primaries, and he could hold dozens of White House breakfasts. He could notify supporters affected by major policy decisions before the public is informed. Little courtesies of this kind are appreciated. Bill Russo, a campaign manager for Gerald Ford, commented on their importance. "Direct mail from the White House is also very impressive, even if it says at the bottom, 'Not printed at government expense.' How often do you see a letter or an invitation from the White House on somebody's wall? If you are flying to California for a fund raiser, call the county chairman in Black Hawk County from Air Force One while you are flying over Iowa." Carter has now fully committed himself to utilize the White House for his re-election. He ordered his cabinet to sell his candidacy and eliminated recalcitrant subordinates. His staff was directed to criticize Kennedy and to emphasize the difficulty the senator was having in defining why he is running and what differentiates him from Carter.

Carter has not done badly with his program in Congress, but his successes — the Middle East treaty, the Panama Canal treaty, and SALT — are not issues that are easily convertible into votes. And they are overshadowed by inflation. The President might enhance his aggressive image by speaking before the Congress and personally leading the struggle for the Strategic Arms Limitation Treaty. He would receive enormous publicity, appear like a true leader of the nation, and, if successful, take the credit. He could use the aura of high drama. If the treaty fails, he could hold Congress responsible.

But inflation is the critical domestic issue. Nothing he can do will have an immediate impact. But politics is as much a matter of postures as it is a matter of realities. The President cannot sharply curtail inflation, but he can forcefully act as if he were attempting to do so. He can play the leader and announce a dramatic effort to halt the rise in prices. He could, for example, launch a nationwide campaign to convince the electorate that his energy program will result in long-term price stability. The message must be "positive results — soon." A very shrewd consultant to George Bush insists Carter needs a dramatic move in early

1980 — whether it is realistic or not makes little difference. "I'd put in wage and price controls. They don't work, but Democrats like them. And we're not talking economics, about whether they deal with causes or symptoms. As far as the public is concerned, they could work politically for the President, and there is something Kennedy couldn't criticize."

No Washington observer believes Carter will be able to stop inflation or successfully claim that he has. His best bet, according to many of the people who manage campaigns, is to find a scapegoat, to blame someone else. The prime targets are obvious: the Congress, OPEC, and the big oil companies. None of these three has much credibility, which suits Carter's purpose.

The Congress is one viable target. To attack Congress, however, is to attack Democrats, who will be needed at the convention. OPEC is an excellent target. Arabs are not a people beloved by most Americans. They appear to be greedy, though, in fact, economically they act as Americans always have, to maximize profit. The best target is the big oil companies, windfall profits, multinational conglomerates gouging the small man. The rhetoric of populism could work well for Jimmy Carter. Certainly it is worth a try, because honest and straightforward defense of his domestic economic policies won't work.

The president must go on the attack. When the campaign began he was the underdog, perceived as weak and ineffectual, while Kennedy was the knight errant. The events in Iran, and not Carter, were responsible for a reversal of roles. After the hostages are released in Iran, Carter would be wise to strengthen his image as a man of force by putting Kennedy on the defensive. Carter can legitimately portray Kennedy as arrogant and pretentious, a candidate who has no reason to run, except personal ambition, because he has agreed with Carter on critical issues for three years.

Despite Kennedy's claim that he reacts well under pressure, the senator has never been involved in a closely contested election. The events at Chappaquiddick suggest that his nerve and judgment are not good under stress. His criticism of the shah was accurate and probably courageous, but in the midst of a national crisis, it was extraordinarily impolitic, indeed stupid.

Edward Kennedy has been a bitter disappointment on the hustings. Though he speaks well from prepared notes, he flounders and is hesitant and inarticulate while speaking spontaneously. He has neither John Kennedy's gift for public presentation nor his gift for rhetoric. His speeches are often puerile, and his command of the language is unsophisticated and stilted. This may reflect the fact that he is one of those American public figures whose self is lost in the persona created by speech writers and ad men.

A piece of Carter's strategy could be designed to shatter this facade. Carter should try to isolate Kennedy and force spontaneous debate, a format in which Kennedy would stand alone. Spontaneous talk was the reason for Kennedy's first major setback during the campaign. Kennedy appeared on national television with Roger Mudd in an informal and unrehearsed conversation on November 4, 1979. After discussing Chappaquiddick, a critical event in Kennedy's life and one he should be well prepared to face, the following exchange took place.

MUDD: Yeah. Do you think, senator, that — anybody really will ever fully believe your explanation of Chappaquiddick?

SENATOR KENNEDY: Well there's —the — the problem is — is from that night I found the — the — the conduct of behavior almost sort of beyond belief myself. I mean, that's why it's been — but that — that's — that's the way it was. That's — that's — that happens to be the way it was. Now, I find it, as I've stated, that I found that the conduct that — in — in that evening and in — in the — as a result of the impact of the accident and the — the sense of loss, the sense of hope, and the — and the sense of tragedy and the whole set of circumstances, that — that the — the — behavior was inexplicable. So I find that those — those — those types of questions, as they apply to that, questions in my soul as well. But that — that happens to be the way it was.

Kennedy's remarks can only be described as incoherent. This is why Carter should confront him face to face. Kennedy made leadership the issue. To lead is to speak. Nothing can tarnish Kennedy's image more as a leader than another confrontation similar to that with Roger Mudd. A campaign manager for George Bush believes that constant harassment of Kennedy could pay handsome returns. "When was the last time he had a tough race? I think he can be rattled. Once you force him out of his set piece, he's in trouble." The expression "set piece" indicates that Bush's manager understands how vulnerable is Edward Kennedy when left solely to his own devices.

We have noted that the American people became significantly more conservative during the seventies, disgruntled at the simultaneous rise in prices and the taxes levied to support a vast welfare program. The mix of economic burden and latent racism is a potent political force. But new conservatives are also preoccupied with the "integrity" of the family, abortion, drugs, crime, busing, homosexual rights, and feminism. We referred to this cluster of attitudes as conservative populism, a rigorous defense of laissez faire coupled with the right of working people to retain a larger portion of their earnings. The conservatives, naturally, seek a drastic cut in public services.

While conservative populism has become a national mood, Edward Kennedy leads the liberal forces in the Senate — more aid for the underprivileged, national health insurance, opposition to expanded military budgets, regulation of multinational corporations — all involving great expense. For Carter's aides, one key to the campaign lies in exploring conservative frustrations and Kennedy's liberalism.

Carter should portray Kennedy as Hoover and Goldwater portrayed FDR and LBJ, stereotype him as a "big spender on the left." Carter should attempt, in other words, not only to isolate Kennedy, but to tag him as a "radical." Some advisors have urged Carter to tell America that Kennedy is a "bleeding-heart liberal," a New Dealer of the 1960s who would bankrupt the country with grandiose schemes of national health insurance, a thoughtless do-gooder who wants bigger government and bigger taxes. One experienced campaigner likes the slogan "Big heart, no brains." Another suggested, "It's our money, not his."

This gambit of isolating and radicalizing the opposition has a long history in American politics. It usually takes the form of a conservative Republican attack on a liberal Democrat (Goldwater-Johnson); in this case we have a liberal Democrat arguing that his opponent is too liberal.

The strategy of isolate and radicalize could be appealing for other reasons. One of the Kennedys' most solid and powerful constituencies through the years has been the blue-collar working class. That constituency has undergone a considerable change. As prosperity filtered down, the blue-collar constituency entered the lower middle class. Their liberalism was then tempered by a reaction to the

radicalism of the sixties — drugs, hippies, and opposition
to the Vietnam War. In the seventies, the working class became even more conservative, in response to higher taxes
to accommodate larger welfare rolls, to "forced busing,"
and to the aura of permissiveness.

Edward Kennedy's name has been prominently associated with some of these causes, and this provides
Carter with a wonderful strategic opportunity, and opportunity to capitalize on conservative populist sentiment. A
well-known pollster described what he thought would be
Carter's best strategy. "At some point you really go after
Kennedy. He's got to try to paint Kennedy as a representative of the far left, of the permissive end of the country.
He has to go back and pick up strong working-class Democrats on a traditional American values–type campaign."
Carter is in a good position to do this. One of the least-
publicized bits of public-opinion data, collected before the
campaign, shows that many more Americans have faith in
Carter's personal morality and integrity than in Kennedy's
character. Carter is in a good position to deal with the issue
of permissiveness. The President and his men can remind
America of Kennedy's cheating at Harvard, of Chappaquiddick, of his scrapes with the police while at law school, and
of his marital troubles.

The President does not need to do this himself. Aides
could talk off the record to hundreds of reporters about
Kennedy, and much of the material would filter through.
To take full advantage of working-class resentment, Carter
would have to select carefully the areas where Kennedy appears to be on the left, highlight these, and "ask" America's
working people if they want a President who will raise
their taxes for vast, dubious schemes of social welfare, a
candidate who defends the civil rights of pornographers

and of homosexuals, and supports proposals that extend the right of abortion. While thus attacking Kennedy, largely to weaken his working-class support, Carter could also deflect a substantial number of Kennedy's Catholic supporters. The issues here would be abortion, busing, and the integrity of the family.

A critique of this kind could be very potent because it is based not only on facts and bread-and-butter issues, but on moral and ethical matters of import, matters that are difficult to compromise or deal with incrementally, precisely because they do involve absolutes. The issue of good and evil cannot be bargained with. Slavery and Prohibition (1920–1933) were the classic moral issues in American politics. We have nothing approaching these in 1980. But the morality of Edward Kennedy is an issue. Abortion is an ethical issue; so are busing and pornography. Welfare can be viewed as an ethical issue if one conceives of it in terms of morally dutiful working people supporting immoral and parasitical idlers.

The significance of the moral dimension for the campaign is that issues with moral content can generate passion, hatred, and adoration. Working-class Democrats who see Kennedy as morally stigmatized cannot possibly believe he is charismatic. The strategy of isolating Kennedy from the working class by stigmatizing him as radical and permissive has the added advantage of demystifying him.

The "big-spender-on-the-left" label that Carter will pin on Kennedy is related to another theme of the campaign, and that is Carter's insistence on the difference between 1960 and 1980. At the dedication of the Kennedy Memorial Library, Carter touched on the issue when he suggested that the eighties, unlike the sixties, is an age of scarce resources and hard choices. The scarcity of energy, coupled with inflation, will lead Carter to campaign on a program of frugality, a campaign that stresses the curtailment of every "unnecessary" program, that contemplates no grandiose schemes at public expense, and that anticipates no rise in taxes. America in the 1980s cannot tolerate the vast expansion of the public sector that John Kennedy and LBJ imagined. This multiple attack is potentially elegant because it could serve so many purposes. It could isolate Kennedy from the blue-collar constituency. It could alienate Catholics from Kennedy. It could potentiate the anger behind conservative populism. It portrays Kennedy as morally questionable and financially irresponsible. The combined effect of these attacks is to demystify Kennedy, tarnish his alleged charisma, and transform him into mortal man. The demystification of a charismatic leader is a bitter blow to true believers. Their adoration may quickly turn into scorn because their hero has fallen.

Some observers believe that the effectiveness of Carter's attack will depend on the resolution of the Iranian crisis. It is likely that Americans will again be preoccupied with inflation, high interest rates, and the price of energy. The emotional "high" of Iran will end, and this letdown, plus the economy, could cause a sharp drop in Carter's popularity. Connally put the matter succinctly: "Carter's polls may fall as fast as they've risen."

There is reason to believe that Governor Connally may be correct. Oil prices are likely to rise again in 1980, and OPEC can easily disrupt the supply of oil if Carter invokes stringent economic sanctions. Recession will become a greater risk as oil prices rise, and inflation, Carter's burden, will continue to plague the President. The hostages and patriotic sentiment have helped Carter to reverse his image as indecisive and ineffectual, but Carter's failure to mitigate the economic crisis may revivify that image. During the crisis, Carter, according to David Broder of the *Washington Post*, ". . . has persuaded the American people that the most prudent course is to blend a demonstration of American restraint with orchestrated international pressure for release of the hostages . . . thus far this policy has not achieved its objective." For Carter, who is seen as a man with good intentions but little political capability, the critical time in Iran may come if his policy of patience is perceived as a failure of will and his caution is taken for impotence.

The Iranian crisis is mercurial. Kennedy has no control over the situation as long as he remains silent, and the President is largely at the mercy of the terrorists. A bold and successful stroke by Carter could permanently damage Kennedy. If the crisis continues for several more months, however, and Carter's tactics fail or the hostages are killed, Carter may be relegated to the ranks of Presidents who served a single term.

In either case, the reaction of the public to the situation in Iran bears upon Kennedy's alleged charisma and Carter's poor image. What is the meaning of Carter's dramatic rise — and possible fall? Public opinion is obviously "soft," attitudes are flexible and unformed, and Democrats and independents are neither so much under the spell of the Kennedy mystique that they have lost their reason nor so disdainful of Carter's performance that they are unwilling to see strength in his command. Kennedy is no longer regarded by Washington pundits as a certain winner, but it would be foolhardy to count him out. He may not be charismatic, his constituency may be less cohesive than it was, but Carter debits are substantial. A long, cold winter and rising household oil prices could revive the Kennedy mystique and bring about another reversal in the polls.

Carter and Kennedy seek what many believe to be the most powerful office in the world. The fact remains, however, that the powers of the President are severely constrained by the Congress, the power of multinational corporations, the self-interest of OPEC, and the truculence of China and the Soviet Union. By examining both presidential power and constraint and what a Kennedy presidency might mean, we can also explore the liberal thrust for social change.

9

A Kennedy Presidency:
Would It Make a Difference?

PRESIDENT CARTER'S first term was distinguished for his role in the Egyptian-Israeli accord and little else. During the past few years, not one major domestic problem was resolved. In fact, urban blight and unemployment spread, the energy crisis and inflation worsened, and the concentration of economic power into fewer multinational corporations accelerated. America is in substantially greater difficulty today than when Carter took office. Washington correspondents, even the more thoughtful ones, usually fail to note that the hallmark of the Carter administration has been a denial of the traditional liberal use of state power on behalf of the less affluent. The Carter administration has been a good friend of big business and the status quo. There is little reason to assume that a second Carter administration would be less negative and less conservative.

What Edward Kennedy would do as president is more difficult to predict, because his legislative record is substantially more liberal than Carter's, yet it is also pragmatic, compromising, and in some ways conservative. Kennedy's career in the Senate runs the ideological gamut from advocacy of a national health plan, a truly radical proposal within the context of American politics, to a revision of the criminal code that is in many ways, if not conservative, at least regressive. Kennedy is heir to the New Frontier, to the liberalism of FDR; he is, unlike Carter, not constrained by a presidential past — in other words he is more free to initiate and innovate. The question of whether a Kennedy presidency will make a difference suggests a dilemma.

Students of the presidency would argue that the success of a Kennedy administration would depend, in part, on his administrative ability, his ability to act as the vigorous chief executive of a large and unwieldy staff. There is some merit to the view that the federal bureaucracy is so proliferated and so fragmented that a president can make a difference only if he can impose his will on senior bureaucrats. Presidents who did make a difference, however, were not only able administrators, but masters of the art of congressional persuasion, leaders of the Congress who instinctively knew when to use finesse (a quiet breakfast at the White House), and when to mobilize fully the powers of the presidency — for example, with a speech on national TV placing responsibility on Congress for the national malaise.

Presidents, however, are not primarily remembered for their administrative skills or congressional relations. Those who have made a difference, those who have altered the course of our history — Jefferson, Jackson, Lincoln, Woodrow Wilson, and FDR — did so because they had a world view, a political posture, an idea, a policy, something of relevance to say. Jefferson's commitment to First Amendment freedoms and free public education did affect American history. Jackson's advocacy of populist politics and Lincoln's advocacy of a national union altered American history. Woodrow Wilson's concept of the League of

Nations prepared the way for the United Nations. Franklin Roosevelt's philosophy of a regulated economy altered the course of American society.

Does Edward Kennedy have anything new to say? Does he have a world view? Does he have an idea? Does the heir to Camelot seek some qualitative change, some grand alteration, or will he, like the other American politicians, be content to initiate only incremental change, change at a pace so slight and so slow that those who control the great multinational corporations will continue to play, in alliance with the defense establishment, a decisive role in the formation of American public policy, a role that reinforces the status quo and maintains the contours of the class system approximately as they are, regardless of who occupies the White House.

We have made Edward Kennedy's record in the Senate available — the struggle for health care, the effort to control corporate mergers, the revision of the criminal code, and liberalism in foreign policy. If the past is prologue to the future, then Edward Kennedy will behave as President much the way he did as senator. He will remain within the confines of American liberalism. He will not seek to alter the flow of power away from the multinational corporations, nor will he reduce the power of the defense establishment to the point where billions of dollars become available for social welfare. National health insurance, in sum, will probably be a prime objective of his administration, and the traditional liberal concern, a limited concern, for the welfare of the poor will be slightly expanded, but not to the point where a shift in economic burdens and economic benefits become political deficits for a Kennedy administration. There will be more programs for the poor, more programs for the ill, more programs to promote the economic opportunity of minority groups, to reduce urban blight, to provide low-cost housing. In other words, the New Frontier and the Great Society will receive some attention, but free enterprise will remain the quintessence of the economic order. The concentration of economic power will not be seriously threatened, and the combination of this free enterprise and this economic power will create a proliferation of the very problems that a Kennedy administration might wish to solve.

Whether Kennedy will be able to control the presidency and the massive bureaucracy is perhaps the least difficult question to answer in terms of his record. Franklin Roosevelt, who dealt with lesser bureaucracies, once lamented, ". . . but the Treasury and the State Department put together are nothing compared with the NA-A-VY. The admirals are really something to cope with — and I should know. To change anything in the NA-A-VY is like punching a feather bed. You punch it with your right and you punch it with your left until you are finally exhausted, and then you find the damn bed just as it was before you started punching."

Harry Truman, speaking of Eisenhower and bureaucracy, was poignant. "Poor Ike; he'll sit there and say 'Do this' and 'Do that' and nothing will happen!" Apparently, Eisenhower as President lived with the fantasy that he was still in the army, for he tried to establish a clear and rigid chain of command along which orders were to pass efficiently down the line. But as Truman predicted, little happened, and Eisenhower left the White House, a classic example of a President who did very little — which, of course, is what big business wants.

The President must not only deal with the vast bureaucratic network composed of almost five million civil servants, he must also contend with the prospect that members of his own cabinet may become his natural adversaries. Most cabinet members have their own power bases and their own constituency, as well as substantial expertise and experience not available to the chief executive. These differences in perspective and in expertise enhance the possibility of a conflict of interest.

A secretary of labor may have more sympathy and closer ties with the leadership of the AFL-CIO, for example, than with his own President. Gerald Ford's secretary of labor, Peter Brennan, resigned in protest over a presidential veto of a labor-sponsored bill (the common-sites picketing bill). Several key people in the Carter administration were forced out last summer because of disagreements with the chief executive.

Presidents have experimented with many techniques to exercise control over the executive branch. The most common has been for the chief executive simply to ignore or deny publicly that internal conflicts exist. A President may appoint a number of highly independent and competent professionals to the cabinet and then discover, as did Carter in the summer of 1979, that many either did not function well, or refused to "play" with the team, or had very different ideas about public policy. There are also personal problems; many good friends or loyal campaign supporters find themselves ill suited for government office. The fraternity induced by a campaign struggle often "forces" the winner to reward his friends, but the scandals and secrets of the past are often made public by the media, and the President finds that yesterday's friend is tomorrow's liability. Carter knows this well, for Bert Lance is under indictment for financial manipulations and Hamilton Jordan is under investigation for the use of illegal drugs.

Students of the presidency agree that the most successful way to deal with the bureaucracy is through the method known as "controlled disorganization," in which assistants, departments, and bureaus have overlapping and conflicting responsibilities and tasks. Disputes constantly arise in the lower echelons of the bureaucracy that must be resolved by higher authority. To deal with these disputes, the President must know where to go for reliable information and whom to trust before making decisions, or better still, he must be able to trust others to make some of these decisions for him. The President, therefore, attempts to surround himself with a hard core of loyalists who stand at the crossroads where information is most likely to flow. The system is not unlike gathering a group of master telephone operators who are able to monitor thousands of calls.

Controlled disorganization appears to be a chaotic non-system, but the President receives numerous and important benefits from it. He can create a network of checks and balances that prevents the growth of arbitrary power centers beyond his control. He can place loyalists at the points where information collects and be made aware of bureaucratic conflicts. However, he must be deft at handling sensitive administrators, because this system maximizes his contacts with them, and therefore also the potential conflict.

Edward Kennedy has had experience with the system of controlled disorganization. As a young senator and observer of the Johnson administration, Kennedy was able to watch a skillful President deal with a burgeoning bureaucracy. He has also used the system with his staff, the largest in the Senate. He often has the parties of a dispute meet with him and present their divergent views, and then he makes decisions based on their input. In this way, options and initiatives that might have been suppressed come to attention. Kennedy has shown a marked interest in the views of lesser members of his staff and has, consequently, been well informed.

The Congress presents a very different set of problems. The President must deal with a byzantine power structure, hierarchies of committee and subcommittee chairmen, many of whom attend constituencies whose interest is antithetical to that of the President. The men and women in Congress who hold power frequently belong to segments of the party that seek to block the President's program. Congressional barriers are numerous and formidable, but the President holds two trump cards: Ever since the thirties, the President initiates the legislative program, and he does have the power to veto acts of Congress.

Despite the powers of the presidential office, Carter's record with the Congress is poor. His key bills on energy were soundly defeated in the Senate and the Strategic Arms Limitation Treaty remains in limbo. It is questionable, with the new Soviet aggression, that SALT will even be an issue in 1980.

Kennedy would be one of the few Presidents in this century to be a "Senate man." He is familiar with the rules of the Senate game. He knows the members who count, the techniques of persuasion, the necessity for give and take. He knows the political predisposition of chairmen and, therefore, what he, as President, can hope to do. This is a great advantage. But the key to his possible success is the warmth and respect that senators have for Kennedy because of seventeen years of hard work.

As a body, however, the Senate, by its very nature and composition, creates problems for the President. The constituency of every senator differs markedly from the President's national constituency. A President who attempts to promote legislation to raise taxes on the major oil companies may be popular with energy-minded citizens, but he will clash with senators from oil-producing states, regardless of political past. Congressmen are under pressure from many private-interest groups, industry lobbyists, and supporters from the home state, interests that basically do not concern the President.

The Senate is a proud group that will fight to protect its prerogatives and its right to obstruct and dissent. Known as "the world's greatest deliberative body," the Senate is organized so that any member who protests a motion can use the filibuster to block Senate proceedings for days. Tedious deliberation and endless bargaining are often required to avoid alienating an important member. Kennedy will face this problem if elected, but he does have experience with the delicacy of Senate coalitions and cloakroom maneuvering.

For Kennedy, a more serious prospect is hostile encounters with his Senate opponents. During his early years in the Senate, Kennedy made enemies by taking a firm stance on controversial "liberal" issues. He also disappointed and angered many colleagues by grossly mishandling his duties as majority whip. Hostility to Kennedy was so great that Senator Byrd of West Virginia soundly defeated Kennedy for whip in a bitter and humiliating fight. As President, Kennedy would have to work closely with his former opponent, now the Senate majority leader. Their relations in recent years have been cordial, however, and ties of party loyalty might overcome personal animosity. Senator Byrd sees the role of majority leader as that of a passive agent of the party rather than as a spokesperson who must influence policy. This should facilitate matters with Kennedy.

Senator Russell Long of Louisiana is another Kennedy adversary who might well relish the chance to frustrate the President. Ever since Kennedy defeated Long for the position of majority whip in 1969, the two have opposed each other on numerous issues. As chairman of the powerful Senate Finance Committee, Long could, if provoked, form a coalition to oppose cuts in the defense budget, the expansion of social welfare programs, or the regulation of big oil.

A favorable coincidence in the electoral cycle may help Kennedy work with Democrats in the Senate. Many liberal Democrats stand for re-election in 1980 in races that are likely to be closely contested. In 1978, three liberal Democrats were defeated, Clark of Iowa, Riegle of Michigan, and McIntyre of New Hampshire. Carter's record was apparently a detriment to their cause. With this in mind, and the remembrance of the Camelot legend, Edward Kennedy's coattails looked very long before the crisis in Iran. In the fall of 1979, dozens of senators and congressmen urged Kennedy to run for the presidency, fearful for their own seats and concerned that the Republicans might gain control of the Senate for the first time since 1954. Carter, at the time, appeared to be more of a detriment than an advantage. These congressmen were also worried that Carter might win the nomination and then do badly in the election.

If Kennedy's coattails were sufficiently strong to make the difference in some senatorial elections, his stock of good will in the Senate would be substantial, and he would be in a good position to demand solid legislative support. A Kennedy landslide, which appeared to be at least a possibility before the Iranian emergency, would guarantee the

new President a honeymoon period considerably longer
than that which many Presidents have enjoyed.

The House of Representatives, on the other hand, would
present Kennedy with a different set of problems and also
some assets he would not enjoy in the Senate. Kennedy's
ties with the leaders of the lower house are intimate. The
Speaker of the House, Tip O'Neill of Massachusetts, was a
close friend of John Fitzgerald Kennedy and has remained
a close friend of Ted Kennedy. O'Neill has always been an
all-out supporter of Kennedy-sponsored legislation. He is
one of the last great ward heelers, one of the last machine
politicians to make it to the very pinnacle of Washington's
power. The tie between O'Neill and the Kennedys is
strengthened by the fact that Tip O'Neill occupies the seat
in the House that John Kennedy occupied before his elevation to the Senate. O'Neill will undoubtedly be one of Kennedy's leading supporters in the House because the
Speaker is not only a staunch party man but also a
member of the liberal wing of the Democratic party. The
powers of the Speaker have been somewhat curtailed in the
last twenty years, but undoubtedly O'Neill remains the single most powerful member of the House, and he would
place his power solidly behind programs sponsored by Edward Kennedy.

The support that Kennedy might receive from the remainder of the House of Representatives is more in question. The average House member is less ideological than
Kennedy and the Speaker, and is customarily elected
largely on the basis of seniority. With 435 members, the
House has many more foci of power than the Senate, many
more opportunities in the flow of legislation for a small
group, or individuals in a position of power, to block or
frustrate the will of the majority or force compromises that

serve the interests of minorities. The fragmentation of power in the House of Representatives is even greater than that in the Senate, and therefore, the possibility of mobilizing the House is substantially less than that of mustering the Senate. The sheer size of the House, the labyrinth of committees and subcommittees, the closer ties of members to the demands of smaller and more particularistic constituencies, increases the likelihood that the President, seeking a national constituency, will find the lower chamber to be more intractable than the Senate, and more concerned with parochial interests.

Kennedy, as President, will need the prestige and the power of the Speaker to advance controversial legislation, such as the national health insurance plan. Tip O'Neill, for example, has had a difficult time developing support for President Carter's programs. O'Neill did manage to organize the House in support of Carter's energy bill, although the bill died in the Senate. He failed, however, to rally the House in 1979 when it refused to grant Carter authority to ration gasoline.

The problem of presidential leadership in the Congress is exacerbated by the fact that American political parties are neither highly disciplined nor ideologically unified. The parties are, rather, loose groups of professional politicians who form temporary coalitions for particular purposes, and then disband, and then unite again. Senators and members of the House are substantially more committed to what they perceive as the needs of their constituency than they are to the rigors of party ideology or party discipline. Neither the majority leader in the Senate nor the Speaker in the House of Representatives is able to punish recalcitrants so as to alter seriously their party commitment. Everybody knows this; therefore there is little fear of political recrimination. For these reasons, presidential leadership remains a high political art.

One critical measure of presidential greatness is the ability of the chief executive to transcend the negative thrusts of the Congress, the power plays that enormously increase the likelihood that the President will become a pawn of the Congress. Carter has failed to mobilize the Congress, and this is one of the reasons why Edward Kennedy campaigns essentially on the slogan of leadership. The argument is that his years in the Senate and his friendship with the House enhance his knowledge of the Congress, and the Congress's knowledge of him, so that the possibility of presidential leadership is real.

The independence and isolation of members of the House from presidential pressure has become much greater in the past decade because members believe, and correctly so, that they, and not the party organization or the presidential coattails, were responsible for their election and reelection. A member of the House is in intimate contact with his constituency. The President of the United States may hardly be aware of its existence. Members of the House, with large personal staffs, are able to deal with thousands of constituency problems, ranging from lost Social Security checks to admission to West Point. It is meticulous attention to these "cases" that cements the bond between the constituency and the member of the House. The member can also flood the constituency with mail, at no cost to himself, maintaining his presence and position. With an independent power base, the average congressman has little to fear from presidential pressure.

The problem of presidential leadership is compounded by the fact that the structure of the House has changed in recent years in favor of younger and more independent mavericks. Throughout most of American history the seniority system was used to determine the chairmen of committees, a system that granted the chairmanship automatically to that member of the majority party with the longest continuous service on the committee. In the mid-seventies, however, a major reform bill shifted some of the chairmen's power to the chairmen of subcommittees, members with substantially less service, and members whose party loyalty was more questionable. Even though this structural change made it more difficult for the Speaker and the President to control the House, the reorganization could help Kennedy because the change in the seniority system has infused the power structure of the House with a larger number of liberal and younger members. The significance of this turnabout in the seniority system is very great. For example, liberal presidents like FDR had overwhelming Democratic majorities to work with in both houses of the Congress, but they had to contend with ultraconservative committee chairmen, and this substantially limited the ability of the majorities to invoke the New Deal. The liberal chairmen of subcommittees in the House today are substantially more inclined to support Kennedy's programs, particularly with Tip O'Neill as Speaker.

Beyond the world of Washington, the question of how Edward Kennedy will be received and what will be expected of him is a complicated one. During the year or two before the election, and even during the part of the campaign that preceded the crisis in Iran, many Washington columnists argued that Edward Kennedy might initiate a modest reform movement. The basis for this expectation is the "unradical," but extensive, character of the Kennedy national health insurance plan, the humanism of his approach to the problem of international refugees, and a long and vigorous commitment to the social welfare of less affluent Americans, particularly the black, Puerto Rican, and Chicano population. The sweeping and humanistic rhetoric of Kennedy's speeches invariably implies the need to bring about a more equitable America, an America in which the power of the multinational corporations is curbed so that smaller businessmen have a chance. This is the rhetoric of the New Deal, of expanded social benefits, of greater economic equality. This is the rhetoric of the underclass.

The rhetoric and the reality of American politics, however, are quite different. Kennedy's record is one of liberal advance and pragmatic retreat, one of liberal innovation and conservative compromising. Kennedy may wish to initiate a reform movement, but the posture of America in the early eighties is a conservative posture. The possibilities of serious reform in America are limited by the power of the multinational corporation, the permanence of the defense establishment, the control of our national politics by OPEC, and the undependable behavior of the Soviet Union and the Muslim world. Reform may be intended, but is not possible.

The possibilities of a major reform movement in America in the mid-eighties are slight for other reasons. The major parties hold similar views of the grand contours of economic and political theory. Liberals and conservatives, Republicans and Democrats are major vehicles for the socialization of the American people into that uniquely American perspective — bourgeois liberalism. The parties and the people are overwhelmingly committed to the belief that the capitalist system is the best way to organize economic experience and that the particular form of American capitalism is best suited to our needs. The parties and the people are committed to the belief that our form of so-called representative government is the best way to organize political experience.

The predictable element of American political life is that tomorrow will resemble today as surely as today resembles yesterday. The political liberalism of Jefferson is still the American creed, and the economic philosophy of Adam Smith, with emendations, dominates economic thinking. American history is remarkably stable; the political and economic philosophy that dominated the Founding Fathers dominates us. The institutional structures they established, the federal system, the separation of powers, and the array of checks and balances, remain the hallmark of American political institutions today. The nation has produced no political philosopher of eminence, no major political movement on the left or on the right, and no revolutionary tradition. If a reform movement were initiated by Edward Kennedy, it certainly would be a movement within the mainstream of America's bourgeois liberalism. The expectation of more is unwarranted.

If Kennedy sought wide-ranging change, however, he might have broader support in the Congress than any President since FDR, and this is because the infusion of liberals and their rise to positions of power greatly augment the ideological resonance of the two branches. The possibility for some qualitative change is enhanced by the fact that several crises now disrupt American politics. The economic squeeze, the energy problem, and the inflationary spiral may be less amenable to traditional liberal solutions. The capitalist economy is obviously somewhat out of hand. Inadequate and very expensive energy is a problem we have never had to deal with before. A growing constituency of environmentalists is making demands upon the Congress that have never been made before, demands that contravene the maximization of profit as the national ethos. It is obvious to some that as Kennedy and Carter compete for the nomination in 1980, the problems that they must deal with have not yielded to traditional solutions.

Throughout our history, proponents of reform have exaggerated their opportunities. The thrust of American politics is toward stability and changelessness. The great American reform movements — populism, progressivism, and the New Deal — did not attempt to introduce socialism or public ownership. Their leaders have never denied a belief in the viability of the capitalist system — indeed, the main thrust of American reform in the twentieth century has been the classic bourgeois ideal of opening the avenues of opportunity to the small man and preserving the capitalist system. The object of American reform has been to create more small capitalists. By so doing, reform movements may appear to be egalitarian when, in fact, their true objective has been the expansion of the capitalist system. Edward Kennedy belongs to this tradition, as did Franklin Roosevelt and TR.

Another reason why there is little likelihood of a major reform movement in the eighties is that the office of the presidency itself is in a state of decline. The next President may wish to initiate a modest reconstruction of American society, but the limitations placed upon the powers of the office seriously diminish his capacity to do so. During the cabinet shakeup in August 1979, the very shrewd columnist Joseph Kraft suggested that the limits on presidential power and the demands of new constituencies were so great that the President of the United States was no longer in a position to alter significantly the course of American life. The powers and majesty of the President foster high expectations in a world that has become increasingly intractable. Vietnam and Watergate have so divided America, so threatened the integrity of the presidential office, that the legitimacy of the office itself is in question. The authority of the presidential office has also been weakened by the failure of John Kennedy's New Frontier and Lyndon Johnson's Great Society. The problems that these programs were designed to mitigate are not only still with us, but with us in ever greater dimension. Decaying cities, inflation, poverty, and enormous problems involved in public assistance are no less virulent in the eighties than they were in the sixties. The rhetoric of John Kennedy and Lyndon Johnson was just that — rhetoric. The dismal failure of the Carter administration with respect to energy and inflation has not added to the authority of the presidency. The question of contemporary politics does not seem to be whether or not a reform movement is in the offing, but whether or not American politics actually works.

For decades American politics was dominated by what Joseph Kraft has called "Big America." He argues that this combination of party organizations, multinational corporations, and unions "gave a President the elements for building coalitions with leaders of either party in the cabinet, the Congress and with mayors and governors . . ." The common goal of economic growth united all of them.

In the 1960s, new pressure groups became a force in American life, groups primarily interested in the quality of life and not the Gross National Product. Kraft refers to groups such as environmentalists, consumer advocates, and minorities as "Little America." The problems for which they seek solutions — nuclear pollution, water pollution and land devastation, quality control of consumer products, and equality of economic and educational opportunity — are substantially more difficult to solve than those directly relating to economic growth. The introduction of these issues, which are supported by not insubstantial pressure groups, has, according to Kraft, "withered the elements of presidential coalition building," because the goals of Big and Little America clash.

The President can no longer count on the continued support of the Congress or the parties, the cabinet or the people. Lyndon Johnson resigned from the White House because of the conflicts engendered by Vietnam. Nixon tried to resolve these conflicts by destroying the groups that opposed him. He attacked the press and television, spied illegally on the opposition party, distrusted members of his own staff, and introduced an unprecedented degree of paranoia into presidential politics. The destruction of the Nixon presidency was due, in part, to the divisiveness introduced by "New America." Ford lowered the expectation of presidential accomplishment and introduced a note of quietude, but not achievement, into the office. Carter has not done better.

"What all this demonstrates," according to Kraft, "is a genuine national problem — a hole in the system. The post-imperial presidency has not yet been defined. It is an office in search of a role." The question of whether or not a Kennedy presidency would make a difference depends upon the degree to which Edward Kennedy could define that role.

If Kennedy were to opt for schemes more grandiose than his predecessors, he would be forced to mobilize and alter public opinion. The quintessential characteristic of American political culture is the unanimity of its bourgeois liberalism, the profound commitment to capitalism and private property, to existing political arrangements, and to anticommunism. This is the American ideology, the fusion of Adam Smith's economics and John Locke's liberal politics — bourgeois liberalism. In its crude form, bourgeois liberalism is the philosophy of the chamber of commerce. To promote a serious reform movement in America, a movement that seeks some qualitative change, the chamber of commerce mentality would have to be challenged seriously, and this is not a real prospect.

Social experimentation in America has always been limited to a veneration of private action and private need. There has been little regard for the effects of this narrow liberty on wider community need. No large-scale qualitative change is possible without the expansion of the concept of community right, with its emphasis on public need. Presidents traditionally implore Americans to think first of the nation and transcend their selfishness. But practical programs are not the result. At least Ronald Reagan has the honesty to portray self-interest as a virtue and thereby voice the true American feeling. Edward Kennedy has at least a dim understanding of the leadership that would be required to initiate a movement favorable to community need. The struggle for national health insurance and the long-term interest in the needs of the urban poor suggest that he may be committed to forging some commitment to mutual assistance, some program that would bind people together in a common enterprise for common benefit.

There is a sense in which Edward Kennedy has understood that private right must be curbed in the interest of wider obligation. In a modest way, he has suggested that a national purpose cannot be possible in a nation where all are committed to private advantage. On the other hand, one must not exaggerate his commitment to community right, for we have seen that free enterprise has always been a priority of his political thought.

The chance that an American President can come to grips

with the energy shortage, inflation, urban decay, inadequate medical care, and the destruction of the environment, depends, in our view, on his willingness to curb "privatism."

The urban historian S. G. Warner, Jr., defined privatism as the organization of society based on the individual's search for wealth. His conclusion was that privatism in America was a major cause of growth at one period of our history and then became a most significant force for the disruption of civil life, for poor planning, dislocation, and the concentration of wealth. Presidents may decry privatism and ask for public action when they appeal to Americans, "Let us work together," but they have steadfastly supported the ethic of private action. Warner examines the meaning of privatism.

> Psychologically, privatism meant that the individual should seek happiness in personal independence and in the search for wealth; socially, privatism meant that the individual should see his first loyalty as his immediate family, and that a community should be a union of such money-making, accumulating families; politically, privatism meant that the community should keep the peace among individual money-makers, and if possible help to create an open and thriving setting where each citizen would have substantial opportunity to prosper. The tradition of privatism has always meant that the cities of the U.S. depended for their wages, employment and general prosperity upon the aggregate success and failures of thousands of individual enterprises, not upon community action.

Americans believe that privatism works well, that the pursuit of self-interest ultimately produces the greatest happiness for the greatest number. But the candidates agree that the nation is in serious trouble. The ethos of privatism obviously is one root of this trouble, although candidates never speculate on the relation of private action to greed and poverty. They avoid the discussion, because this perspective is beyond them, or because it has the ring of socialism. American communities are still a "union of money-making, accumulating families," and American society reflects this today. The American system is a competitive and hostile system, a system in which private gain is a dominant motif.

Leadership, to be meaningful in the eighties, must confront and curb privatism. The first task of a President who would lead, in this sense, is to define new national goals that reflect a public purpose. The second task is to educate the Congress and the public.

Edward Kennedy has some skills in the art of public exhortation. He has moved the Senate on occasion, particularly when speaking of national health and the plight of Asian refugees. He has speech writers of quality who can argue closely and support their arguments with substantial data. Their ability to make complex problems understandable and their capacity to utilize language that is both persuasive and appropriate to a presidential candidate would enhance Kennedy's ability to raise grave questions about the foundations of American culture.

The technical skills necessary for a major effort to alter public opinion in America are available to Kennedy. A huge and talented staff, access to fine academic minds, and endless political contacts could be mobilized to make a critique of privatism and the thrust of existing public policy. These skills, however, are useless unless Kennedy redefines his purpose and his goals, his aspirations and his overall plan for America. Seventeen years in the Senate suggest that Edward Kennedy is not prepared for an undertaking of this magnitude. No doubt, he is among the more pro-wealth and power, or reorienting the nation's goals by creating attitudes critical of privatism and favorable to communalism, then Edward Kennedy will not be catalogued among the great American Presidents. He might succeed in expanding the benefits available to the less fortunate. He might manage to increase the monies available for college loans. He may even extend the quality of medical care. But the problems of America will not be solved by the traditional bread-and-butter politics of liberal Democrats.

When John Kennedy was assassinated and when Lyndon Johnson completed his tenure, wealth in America was more concentrated than it had been, the power of multinational corporations was greater than ever before, the class system was no less stratified, many inner cities were uninhabitable, and the thrust of American life was still characterized by acquisition and greed, competition and callousness. There is little reason to believe, when Carter completes his second term or Kennedy his first, that the situation would be different.

If it were actually possible for Edward Kennedy to promote major qualitative changes, we would complete our analysis by suggesting that Kennedy was an able and hard-working senator, carefully prepared and well staffed, open to opinion and receptive to talent, occasionally willing to question liberal formulas, and that therefore, he might attempt a modest reconstruction of American society, a reconstruction that moderated the impact of privatism.

But such a reconstruction presumes the presence of a political and social theory that could serve as an alternative to bourgeois liberalism. None exists at the moment. What passes for political thought in America, the fusion of

Adam Smith and John Locke, has long been a national cliché.

Edward Kennedy or, for that matter, Jimmy Carter or any other presidential candidate is highly unlikely to break the ideological mold. To ask whether a Kennedy presidency will make a difference is to ask, essentially, whether any man or woman in the White House can deal with increasing challenges to our traditional thinking and methods of operation.

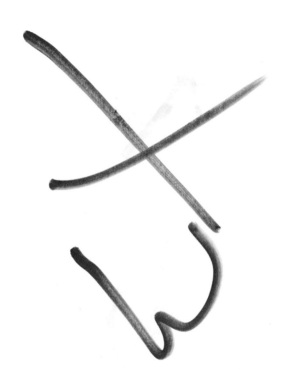